"Debra Laaser's latest book deliv
message—you can not only surviv
trauma. What makes this book so
simply describing the important no
and gives you gentle prompts and e×
one simple step at a time. This book is a blessing for anyone who
has suffered from trauma and is hoping to transform their life."

Daniel G. Amen, MD, author of *Change Your Brain,*
Change Your Life

"Deb shares her intimate and powerful thirty-year personal journey in this book, filled with practical tools for anyone ready to take
their next right step on their path from trauma to transformation!"

Tim Clinton, EdD, LPC, LMFT, president, American Association
of Christian Counselors, and cohost, *Dr. James Dobson's Family Talk*

"*From Trauma to Transformation* takes the reader on a journey of
learning how to maximize betrayal's chaos and pain as a stimulus
for Spirit-led growth. Not because change is required or caused the
spouse to make bad choices but rather because pain has opened
a door, a chance to do things differently. While set in the arena of
sexual betrayal, this book is going to prove helpful to all who are
attempting to work through any trauma. Deb helps you learn to
live daily with the tension of both/and as you practice 'the last
of human freedoms—to choose one's attitude in any given set of
circumstances' (Viktor Frankl). This is no trite self-help. This is a
deep dive, no-holds-barred, gentle journey with the Holy Spirit.
I just wish it had been available when I first started working with
my couples many years ago!"

Dave Carder, MA, MFT, author of *Torn Asunder*
and *Anatomy of an Affair*

"In *From Trauma to Transformation*, Debra Laaser masterfully
leads her readers like a seasoned guide on a challenging journey.
She does so with empathy, understanding, and integrity and has
the courage to walk her own path while also helping light the way
for others. Her ability to weave biblical, personal, and clinical
dimensions of trauma, posttraumatic growth, and transformation provides orientation and stability to an often turbulent and
frightening process. I can think of no more trustworthy guide for
the journey than Debra Laaser!"

David E. Jenkins, PsyD, professor and clinical director
of PsyD program at Liberty University

"Over the past twenty years, our friend and colleague Debbie Laaser has proven herself time and again to be one of the most important thought leaders and practitioners in our field. After reading *From Trauma to Transformation*, we're convinced that God has used Debbie to pen what will surely become a classic on how to move from merely surviving to truly thriving in post-traumatic growth. If you're hurting and searching for the kind of godly wisdom and practical insights that can transform your life, then we invite you to read this book and follow the caring, gentle voice of your new mentor."

Michael and Christine Leahy, co-CEOs of BraveHearts

"Debra writes from the heart. Readers will sense her compassion as she vulnerably weaves her story into a process of embracing betrayal trauma while gently encouraging growth amid the pain. She encourages readers to hold the perspective of a "gentle observer" as she outlines a path, "the next right step," to lead partners on a personal journey of growth as they draw closer to self and to God. As Debra states, 'become better, not bitter from betrayal.' Choose to read this book if you are looking for a way through the anguish of betrayal, and you desire to strengthen yourself and your spiritual life."

Marcus R. Earle, PhD, LMFT, clinical director
of Psychological Counseling Services

"There is more to trauma than just surviving. In *From Trauma to Transformation*, Laaser focuses on helping readers thrive following traumatic events and other adverse life experiences. Laaser takes the concept of posttraumatic growth beyond a theoretical idea and makes it a tangible, transformative process. She does not dismiss the painful reality of trauma but delivers practical, faith-focused suggestions and exercises that lead to transformed relationships with yourself, others, and God following trauma and adverse life experiences."

Elizabeth Griffin, MA, LMFT, and David Delmonico, PhD

"Out of the crucible of her own pain and trauma, Debra gently leads the reader through wise insight and practical experiences along a path to transformation and empowerment."

Dr. Clifford and Joyce Penner, authors of *The Gift of Sex*
and other resources that promote healthy sexuality
within faith-based communities

FROM TRAUMA

TO

Transformation

Other Books by the Author

*Shattered Vows: Hope and Healing for Women
Who Have Been Sexually Betrayed*

*Seven Desires: Looking Past What Separates Us
to Learn What Connects Us*, coauthored with Mark Laaser

*A Toolkit for Growth: Practical Recovery Tools
for Individuals and Couples,* coauthored with Mark Laaser

FROM TRAUMA

TO

Transformation

A PATH TO HEALING AND GROWTH

DEBRA LAASER

Revell

a division of Baker Publishing Group
Grand Rapids, Michigan

Published by Revell
a division of Baker Publishing Group
PO Box 6287, Grand Rapids, MI 49516-6287
www.revellbooks.com

Printed in the United States of America

Library of Congress Cataloging-in-Publication Data
Names: Laaser, Debra, 1951– author.
Title: From trauma to transformation : a path to healing and growth / Debra Laaser.
Description: Grand Rapids, MI : Revell, a division of Baker Publishing Group, [2022] | Includes bibliographical references.
Identifiers: LCCN 2021053674 | ISBN 9780800741990 (casebound) | ISBN 9780800738037 (paperback) | ISBN 9781493431878 (ebook)
Subjects: LCSH: Pain—Religious aspects—Christianity. | Suffering—Religious aspects—Christianity. | Interpersonal relations—Religious aspects—Christianity.
Classification: LCC BV4909 .L25 2022 | DDC 248.8/6—dc23/eng/20220107
LC record available at https://lccn.loc.gov/2021053674

Unless otherwise indicated, Scripture quotations are from THE HOLY BIBLE, NEW INTERNATIONAL VERSION®, NIV® Copyright © 1973, 1978, 1984, 2011 by Biblica, Inc.® Used by permission. All rights reserved worldwide.

Scripture quotations labeled AMP are from the Amplified® Bible (AMP), copyright © 2015 by The Lockman Foundation. Used by permission. www.Lockman.org

The names and details of the people and situations described in this book have been changed or presented in composite form in order to ensure the privacy of those with whom the author has worked.

This publication is intended to provide helpful and informative material on the subjects addressed. Readers should consult their personal health professionals before adopting any of the suggestions in this book or drawing inferences from it. The author and publisher expressly disclaim responsibility for any adverse effects arising from the use or application of the information contained in this book.

Baker Publishing Group publications use paper produced from sustainable forestry practices and post-consumer waste whenever possible.

22   23   24   25   26   27   28   7   6   5   4   3   2   1

To my beloved husband, Mark,
who used his second chance to be
transformed from trauma,
and in so doing helped me be
transformed from mine.

Contents

Contents

Introduction

THIS IS A BOOK ABOUT HOPE. Hope that as you face traumatic life events now or in the future, you'll know you have the choice to move through adversity and become stronger, with richer relationships and a deeper spiritual life. And as you grow and change, you may alter your priorities in life and find new opportunities for meaningful and passionate living.

Yes, despair and growth can coexist. Your life is not wasted when you face tragedy. It can be hard, *and* it can lead you into a journey of learning. Two psychologists, Richard Tedeschi and Lawrence Calhoun, have researched this apparent paradox of growth after a traumatic event and labeled it *posttraumatic growth*.[1]

I have been in recovery for many years. What that means is that over thirty years ago, the truth about my husband's sexual addiction was exposed, and Mark and I were both catapulted into a program of surviving. We called it our "crash and burn," because it seemed that everything in our fifteen-year marriage was destroyed. Of course, today I know that is not a truth. It was, however, the filter that dominated my thinking and responding at the time. Recovering some sense of sanity and calm was paramount. Our counseling and therapy groups brought pieces of that each week. The process soon became more transformational, though.

We learned new information, we started changing behaviors, and we developed hope that our future could be different. A more accurate description of these past thirty-plus years is that I have been transforming.

To *recover*, to return to life as it was—living in secrets, coping in our own ways when life was hard, lacking safety when we tried to talk with each other—was not what we really wanted. Our lives after our crash and burn were about changing the way we lived, especially changing our character. Mark and I were morphing into something new. We were transforming. I decided to abandon the word *recovery* many years ago. It is a term used by many people who are working through difficult life situations or addictions, but it seemed an inadequate and limiting way to describe the ultimate outcome of experiencing growth. I did not want to recover my old life. I wanted a new life, a different life. I wanted to *transform* through trials to become more of the person God created me to be.

For over twenty years, I have had the privilege of working with women who have been relationally betrayed—either emotionally, sexually, or both—in a committed relationship. I have walked alongside these women as their counselor at Faithful & True, the counseling center Mark and I cofounded. I have also led therapy groups in which many of these women participated. In the sanctity of these settings, women shared their stories and struggles. They learned practical steps to change beliefs and behaviors to become better women.

This book captures the practical lessons I have both learned and taught along the way in my personal and professional life—because they help, they work. I never was aided much by encouraging words alone, even though they may have carried a lot of truth. "You will be better because of this!" "You're a strong person; I know you'll get through this." "It just takes time." "Turn it over to God." Although these were truthful statements, I needed something to bring home with me to do *today*. A new thought. A new behavior to try. A book to read. An assignment, of sorts. I like to give assignments, maybe because I liked having them myself. I have always liked something tangible to work on. I am assuming you may too. This book is full of assignments; I call them "next right steps." Small increments for progress. These are doable things to try, even if your life is full and you have little time.

The lessons you'll learn here come from the practical changes I've made during my thirty-plus years of "working on myself." These insights began when I sought to heal from the trauma of betrayal and then continued well beyond that trial, as I loved who I was becoming. I am a different and better person today because of these changes. I am not perfect. I know there will always be something more to work on while I am on this earth. It is the dress rehearsal for my life in my heavenly home. But this process has allowed me to face other adversity with more tools, as we say in the counseling world. I have more truths and practical steps for surviving, and eventually thriving, from difficulties, losses, and pain. That is what I want for you too as you read this book.

This book builds on my first book, *Shattered Vows*, which is a look at the first steps after discovering relational betrayal in your committed relationship. This book gives you practical ways to take trials, trauma, and adversity and use them for positive change in *you*. For healing, I sometimes say. You need to want change in your life, or at least relief from pain, if you want to experience transformation instead of being a victim. A victim waits for everything to fall into place or for others to do the work. A victim might believe because someone else hurt them, that person should be responsible for making it better. You could get stuck there. If you want to learn from pain, you will need to work at it. That sounds strange as I type it, yet it is true. You will need to take responsibility for wanting to heal and become a better person even amid or despite hard things that happen to you.

If you sign up for that, I can help you. It is your choice.

Alcoholics Anonymous (AA) has some of the best, most concise sayings for changing your life. This is one I love: "Take what you need and leave the rest." No one has all the answers. I would not want you to agree with all I say. I am only one person who has worked at finding peace in the midst of life's hardships. I know some things because I have been through some things. *And* I don't know everything. Take what fits and listen carefully to how the Holy Spirit is guiding you. (I will talk more about how to do this in a later chapter.)

In this book you'll learn practical steps to becoming a new person, the person God created you to be. The best version of yourself. You have been gifted a life of love, talents, passion, and purpose by our God who is all-loving. He wants you to thrive. He wants you to live in his peace. He wants you to love and be loved without limitations. Will you choose to live loved? This book can help you with your journey. I know we often use the word *healing* to describe this journey. Again, I like *transforming* better. Each time I've moved through some trial, it has changed me. It has transformed me. I believe it is making me a better person, more Christlike in my character and more knowing of God, who loves me unconditionally. I have a long way to go, *and* I am committed to work at it daily.

I love hearing stories of people who have been through difficult times and are on the thriving side of those stories. In church, people often share testimonies of overcoming tragic experiences or disease. We also read about sports stars who miraculously overcame a painful accident and are now excelling in the arena. These stories can give us hope for our own story. Something transformational evolved from something traumatic. Just as he promised, God does not waste people's pain. He redeems it.

I am writing this book in the middle of another traumatic season of life. My husband recently died from cancer after bravely battling a disease that we were told was very manageable. I am now facing a new challenge. I counsel, teach, coach, and accompany women who are on this kind of journey. I have acquired many practical ways to transform trauma because I know that trauma and transformation can coexist. Yet this is the most traumatic experience of my life. It is hard to be a widow. I am not sure yet what my transformation will look like. I am surviving, *and* I anticipate that a season of thriving will one day be mine. I am an avid believer that God will redeem this pain too.

With a book contract to attend to, it occurred to me that maybe all my great ideas about transforming trauma would come from a more sensitive place since I was in the *middle* of difficult times. Maybe my writing would have more depth. I am still not sure. This thought was just laid on my heart (from the Holy Spirit, I believe) as I struggled to get writing.

We have also been living through the tragic COVID-19 pandemic. The world has shut down in ways it never has before. We have new language: social distancing, the dangerous curve, exponential growth, experimental drugs, PPE, Zoom. It changed the way we live in a matter of a few months. Especially in its early days, there was no certainty of the future. We were all trying to figure out how to survive in this traumatic time. Will there be transformation in this crisis too?

If we believe God does not waste our pain, then in all these circumstances, we can hope to grow our character. My expertise is helping women who have been relationally betrayed, but I know for sure that the principles and practices I want to share with you here apply to transforming anything traumatic.

Because I am now more than thirty years past my relational trauma, I tend to forget those first weeks and months of surviving and being filled by devastating information. What I usually remember is what eventually happened: the people who led me out of Egypt, so to speak, and the transformation that began to appear in every nook and cranny of my life, not because of the betrayal but because of the journey the betrayal led me to. My beliefs about myself, my husband, and the world were shattered. I needed a lot of help. Thankfully, help arrived quickly. I was literally carried into a new world of possibilities. I know today God was right in the middle of all those happenings.

I tend to focus on the part of my story when my life got better and richer. I want "better and richer" for you as well. It is possible you are not yet ready to move beyond a chapter of great pain. That is all right. You will know when you are ready to embrace the possibility that trauma and transformation can coexist. God does not want to waste your pain. If you are willing to give him a chance, he will use adversity to teach you many things, to change the very character of who you are, and to draw you closer to him.

1

The Pain of Being in Pain

Although the Lord gives you the bread of adversity and the water
of affliction, your teachers will be hidden no more; with your own
eyes you will see them. Whether you turn to the right or to the left,
your ears will hear a voice behind you, saying, "This is the way;
walk in it."

Isaiah 30:20–21

STRESSFUL AND TRAUMATIC LIFE EVENTS can create great suffering, both physical pain in your body and psychological pain—
shattered beliefs about yourself and the world. If you are going to
heal trauma, you must address all pain. Trauma delivers a lot of
suffering. You can be victimized by it and live a life of bitterness
and survival, or you can overcome it and live a life of thriving. This
book will help you move through trials and adversity so that one
day you can say you are growing and thriving.

I did not learn how to deal with hard things growing up. When I
look back, I would say that my life, in general, was extremely good.

Very pain-free. *Dramatic, frightening, unstable, dangerous*—those are not words I would use to describe my home. And yet, I know there were troubling things I had to navigate when I was a child: polio when I was three, a move to a new school with new friends when I was five, a mean teacher when I was in third grade, getting glasses in fourth grade, a twin sister who seemed to be far more popular in junior high, when things like that mattered. The list goes on. I bet you are thinking, *That is nothing compared to what I lived with!* And you may be right. It can be tempting to compare the challenges of our lives.

As a little girl, I noticed there were ways to avoid pain. Not talking about trouble seemed to work. Waiting for time to heal pain was also a strategy. Humor could deflect a painful situation. I was told that everybody had to accept things they did not like; it was part of getting to the better things. And I was told that if you were good, bad things would not happen to you. My experiences told me differently. Despite my efforts to avoid trouble and pain, they were still there.

We live in a culture that wants us to avoid pain. Store shelves are filled with medications to eliminate painful symptoms. Endless commercials promote new drugs to reduce our aches and pains. Our medical professionals treat physical symptoms so we do not have to be in pain. Most days, that is a relief to know. With disease and surgeries and failing bodies, I am eternally thankful to know we have tools available to help reduce pain, even if I fast-forward through all those commercials. As I grow older and watch more people I know face end-of-life situations, I am reminded that in many cases, it will not be easy. Jesus's death is still hard to fathom. I do not like the movies that depict it and find it too difficult even to watch. I am quite sure I will want drugs when my time comes. I was glad there was morphine for Mark at the end of his life. It was agonizing to watch, and I wanted him to be out of pain. It is not all bad that our culture wants to medicate physical pain and make life more comfortable.

What is important, though, is exploring what you learned about how to manage life when it got difficult. When people were abusive or you were missing things you needed, what did you do? We all began to learn these lessons from those around us when we were small children. Coping is a term many counselors use. I will talk more about coping in a later chapter, but for now, know that coping is a tool used to protect you from or medicate your pain.

A Brief History of Treating Pain and Suffering

Stephen Joseph, a researcher and professor of psychology at the University of Nottingham, summarizes the development of modern psychology in his book *What Doesn't Kill Us*.[1] He explains that in the early twentieth century, the medical model focused on how to relieve people of their physical symptoms and distress. Many advances were being made that contributed to reducing physical pain in the body. At this same time, Sigmund Freud, a medical doctor in Vienna, introduced *psychoanalysis*. It was the birth of the field of psychology. The goal was to bring the unconscious to the conscious to understand behaviors. As a medical doctor, Freud focused on relieving troubling symptoms in his clients, not with medications but with conversation.

An exception to the early focus on relief of stressful symptoms was Viktor Frankl, a psychiatrist and psychotherapist who survived the Holocaust during World War II. His study of survivors eventually led him to write about the meaning in suffering in *Man's Search for Meaning*. Frankl's theories became known as *logotherapy*, suggesting that the most powerful drive for all human beings was to find meaning in life. He noted that one can find meaning in three different ways: (1) by creating a work or doing something good for someone; (2) by experiencing something significant or interacting with someone who profoundly affects you; or (3) by the attitude you have when faced with suffering. Frankl believed that despair was experienced when suffering had no meaning. He saw that there were two sides to suffering, noting that there was nothing inherently good *in* adversity, but perhaps there could be something good to extract *out* of adversity.[2]

During the post-WWII era, the field of psychology continued to emerge, and other psychologists began to study the factors that contributed to well-being and growth. Abraham Maslow developed his theory of self-actualization and also saw the both/and of suffering. He proposed that the most important learning came from traumas and tragedies because they forced people to look at new perspectives. The pain from trauma was painful *and* it was good.[3]

A great advance in medicine occurred after the Vietnam War, when posttraumatic stress disorder (PTSD) was finally named as a medical diagnosis. Veterans returning with painful physical and psychological symptoms were diagnosed with PTSD and treated to reduce symptoms of anxiety, nightmares, sleeplessness, panic attacks, intrusive and recurring thoughts, hypervigilance, and dissociation. Once again, well-being was synonymous with eliminating physical symptoms that caused suffering. There was a growing belief that triggering events would inevitably lead to PTSD from which patients would never recover.[4] Controlling symptoms would be the best anyone could do.

While there were threads of believing suffering and growth could coexist, the medical model dominated psychological treatment until the late twentieth century. This model focused on the goal of eliminating symptoms. At that time, psychological health was simply defined as the absence of suffering, without focusing on the potential of growth from adversity. However, psychologists began separating themselves from the field of psychiatry (a component of the medical model), especially with the birth of positive psychology in 1999. Martin Seligman, the newly elected president of the American Psychological Association, founded the movement with a desire to study the science of human strengths, virtues, happiness, and what makes life worth living. The movement did not advocate that only positive aspects of living were important to well-being. Psychologists were recognizing it was naïve to think a life could have no sadness or misfortune; rather, the pursuit of happiness must include learning how to live with and learn from adversity.[5]

At about the same time that positive psychology was starting to focus on the benefit of adversity, professors Richard Tedeschi and Lawrence Calhoun from the University of North Carolina published the Posttraumatic Growth Inventory. This assessment tool measured the positive legacy of trauma.[6] Using this tool, they and other researchers found that growth was evident in many traumatic life situations, including loss of loved ones, diagnosis of terminal illness, divorce, childhood abuse, wartime tragedies, and natural disasters.

Posttraumatic Growth

I loved exploring the clinical work of Tedeschi and Calhoun when I was in graduate school. Their research in posttraumatic growth supported the journey I had been on through betrayal. I knew that it had been a traumatic season in my life. As I describe in *Shattered Vows*, one day I thought life was going along rather well—I had a husband grounded in his career and three healthy children; we were involved in church, school, and with our neighbors; we had supportive families—and then disclosure of Mark's secret life spun everything out of control as if we had been tossed about by a tornado. The consequences for both of us were extreme. Our world was broken into pieces. It was hard to imagine that anything good could come from the devastation.

Some said I would never recover from such trauma, yet I did. In time, I grew stronger, my relationships became deeper and more authentic, and my relationship with God was more personal and authentic. I was different. I was better for the crisis. Eventually, I was even grateful for the opportunity this trial brought me to do life differently. That does not mean I had to be thankful for the trial itself. The message of posttraumatic growth is a both/and: you can hate the pain, *and* you can love the transformation. Tedeschi and Calhoun consistently found that we can be transformed by trauma—if we choose. So I, too, propose we can become better, not bitter, from betrayal or any other adversity in our lives. With supportive resources and a desire to find meaning in your trial, you can not only survive but thrive. In the research I led, which was published in 2017, women who had been relationally betrayed and found counseling, community, truth-telling, and spiritual support also consistently experienced posttraumatic growth. They grew stronger as individuals, experienced richer relationships, changed priorities in their lives, embraced new opportunities, and experienced spiritual growth. Our research of over two hundred women indicated that those who had experienced the greatest trauma in their betrayal also experienced the greatest growth.[7] That result gives hope for anyone facing betrayal trauma.

This newfound theory of growth after adversity, birthed in the mid-1990s, led to more research and findings for the growth that followed traumatic life experiences. Joseph surmises that posttraumatic stress is a natural and normal process of adapting to the shattered beliefs that accompany any adversity, and it is the beginning of a transformative journey. "Posttraumatic stress is the engine of transformation—of a process known as posttraumatic growth. . . . It is in the struggle to make sense of a traumatic event that growth can take hold."[8]

While the field of psychology only began discussing the topic of posttraumatic growth in the late twentieth century, Scripture has been telling us these truths all along:

> We also glory in our sufferings, because we know that suffering produces perseverance; perseverance, character; and character, hope. (Rom. 5:3–4)

> Consider it pure joy, my brothers and sisters, whenever you face trials of many kinds, because you know that the testing of your faith produces perseverance. Let perseverance finish its work so that you may be mature and complete, not lacking anything. (James 1:2–4)

God's Word tells us we are to rejoice in our suffering and be glad about our trials, for he is going to grow us up in some new ways during these times. That was a difficult concept for me to accept, especially when, as a girl, I mostly learned to avoid difficult times and rejoice only in the good ones. Nothing prepared me for what was sure to come—troubles (John 16:33). And I had to prepare myself to learn something while despairing too! In my family, that sounded like pure nonsense. My counseling journey through relational betrayal and my subsequent growth, however, proved those Scriptures to be true. Rather than ask, "Why me?" I was learning to ask God, "What would you have me learn?"

My clinical training and my personal journey through trauma merged, validating the spiritual journey I knew I was on. I experienced many aha moments. Yes, what my research was finding was exactly what I had personally experienced. God does have a plan for our troubles. Growth can emerge through tribulation. Pure passion and purpose sprouted in me and led to my master's thesis and future research in the field of posttraumatic growth. God will not waste your pain or mine. While he does not cause us pain for the sake of having trials, he will use our trauma to grow us up to be the best version of the beautiful person he created each of us to be. Trauma and transformation can coexist.

The Myth of the Perfect Family

At our counseling center, we remind our clients that there is no such thing as a perfect family. Historically, the clinical world talked about some families as being dysfunctional, and out of that dysfunction children were hurt and abused. Furthermore, neglect and abuse led children to cope in unhealthy ways and choose behaviors or substances to medicate that pain, which in turn hurt others. So parents, especially, got blamed for not being better parents. And if you came to counseling for help and said you came from a good family, you were often told you were probably in denial. It was a no-win situation for those, like me, who'd lived with a lot of love and safety in their home.

I believe differently today about parents and families. We live in a fallen world, as described in Genesis. Adam and Eve found themselves in a mess when they did not obey God, and we have all been scrambling ever since to try to rid ourselves of the sin nature we acquired when that happened. In other words, life will not be perfect. None of us will live perfectly. We will not parent perfectly. We will not love perfectly. We will not protect perfectly. Therefore, no one can really say they come from a perfect family.

It is also probably true that no one became a parent to purposefully hurt their children. I cannot think of any parent I know who would have ever said, "I think I will have children, but I know I will not love them or try to take care of them." No, we all think it will be wonderful, until it gets hard. And we had no idea how hard it can get some days. For many, the lack of money, time, and talents it takes to raise little ones with constant love and attention begins to blur with all the challenges and troubles of life. And the pain in these big folks spills over to their little ones. And now the children also have pain they must learn to manage in some way. A generational pattern begins, as we often learn and repeat from those who raised us—at home, in church, at school, or in our neighborhoods. How we manage pain is a big generational pattern that is often not healthy.

If there are no perfect families, then we all had some good things and some hard things come out of our early life experiences. This does not need to be judged or blamed. It just is. Exploring those experiences will help you know more about what shaped and formed you. Why do you believe what you do? Why do you do what you do when you are mad? When you are sad? When you are afraid? Why do you drink when you are lonely, but someone else works like crazy? Why do you scream and threaten when you are angry, but another person withdraws and gets quiet? These things are important to know if you have any interest in growing to become the best version of yourself. The emotions of sadness, fear, anger, and loneliness create pain within your heart. If you do not acknowledge they are there and choose a healthy behavior to manage them, you will find an unhealthy way to cope. To paraphrase Maya Angelou, we all need to figure out how to be *in* pain without being *a* pain.[9]

The Myth of the Perfect Relationship

When you leave your imperfect family, another story develops for many of you. You find Prince Charming, a person who appears to be all you need to live pain-free! He is there for all your needs. In fact, during the beginning of any relationship, there is enormous focus on taking care of the needs of the other. It creates bonding as you depend on each other. You are the perfect one, perhaps the only one, who has ever met needs so flawlessly. It is sweet . . . for a while.

In all committed relationships, the season of infatuation ends. You start experiencing differences. You did not know he was so messy; you love an organized house. Or he wants to be sexual every day, more frequently than you do. Or you like to go to bed early, and he loves to stay up late. Differences start to show up in all areas of life. You may also need to get back to everyday responsibilities like work, school, or parenting. And neither of you has time to attend to every need of the other. Sooner or later, you will disappoint each other, and "perfect" no longer describes you. The shattered dreams of an ideal relationship create pain too. Many people who do not explore their disappointments will reach for quick, unhealthy solutions to get their needs met. Pornography, affairs, alcohol, drugs, excessive work, sex, hobbies, sports, computer games, and many other choices can be used to medicate those feelings. Pain can lead to some very unhealthy lifestyles and prevent us from enjoying the fullness of life.

What You Have Learned from Pain

Some of you have experienced other pain too: death of a loved one, illnesses with physical pain, sexual and/or physical abuse, divorce of parents, natural disasters, accidents, financial loss, broken trust, betrayal, injustice, and trauma of various kinds. While life can offer many wonderful experiences and memorable events, it is also filled with a lot of pain.

No wonder we hate pain. We do not know if we will be all right. We do not know if it will ever end. We do not know who we can trust. We do not know if we are the problem. We do not know how to fix it. We do not know a lot of things, and frankly, that can drive us crazy. When we go through painful situations, we create a lot of distorted beliefs about ourselves, others, and the world. These thoughts or beliefs cause great emotional pain. Ronnie Janoff-Bulman, in *Shattered Assumptions*, states, "there are times when one's fundamental assumptions are seriously challenged, and an intense psychological crisis is induced. These are times of trauma."[10] She summarizes the influencing power of our thoughts and beliefs:

> It is how an event is understood that ultimately determines whether it will be traumatic or not. . . . People respond differently to potentially threatening situations, and this is also the case with life events. Those events that seem most overwhelming do not produce a traumatic response in every survivor, and other life events that may not be considered very threatening may, in fact, produce a traumatic response in some survivors. It always comes down to a question of interpretation and meaning. What does this event mean to the victim?[11]

I found this to be true in my research with betrayed women too. Shattered beliefs were highly correlated to the severity of trauma a woman experienced.[12] It will be important for you to know what

26

you believe about your painful situations. You began to believe things about yourself and others as life happened. You most likely were not aware you were creating meanings or core beliefs about yourself and others, yet that is what you were doing. For instance, if your mom or dad neglects you, you may start to believe *I don't matter.* If people criticize you often, you may believe *I can never do anything right.* If your classmates rarely choose you for projects, you may believe *I am stupid.* If you are bullied in school, you may believe *I am defective and unacceptable.* If you need to take medication for a medical condition, you may believe *There is something wrong with me.* If someone jokes that you were the "oops" baby, you may believe *I am not valued or wanted.* If someone abuses you, you may believe *I am not safe in this world.* If you are relationally betrayed, you may believe *I will never be able to trust my husband again* or *I will not be able to take care of myself if I choose to leave.*

You form beliefs and interpretations all the time. There are hundreds of them inside you that create filters for how you see yourself and others. Many of these beliefs are not true; they are just the "story in your head." You often do not think about these beliefs; they just direct your life in an autopilot way, unless you stop and examine them. It is important to know that what you believe will create your feelings. If you believe you do not matter, you may feel sad. If you believe you can never do anything right, you may feel angry, frustrated, or guilty. If you believe you are not valued, you may feel ashamed, lonely, or sad. If you do not feel safe, you may feel scared. All your beliefs will trigger an emotional response. Therefore, if you want to work on healing emotional pain, it will be important to explore your beliefs and update them to what is true. Are you stupid? Are you not worthy or valued? Do you mess up all the time? Can you be safe? Many of the beliefs you live with are simply distorted. They are not true.

Let me say that again. They. Are. Not. True.

If you are relationally betrayed, you might assume you will never be able to trust your spouse again. You may believe you are not loved. You may assume he is not the person you married. You may perceive everyone in the world will judge you if they find out. The pandemic also led to many varied assumptions: *I may die from this if I am not careful to protect myself. Everyone is making a big deal out of nothing. The world will never be a safe place again. We just need to be patient and wait this out. Life will never be the same.* When I became a widow, assumptions pulsed through me too: *I am young and will have to live alone for many years. The world is focused on couples, so now I do not fit in. It has been over a year; I should probably be further along with my grief.* We all create assumptions when we are in trials. Often they are not truth. In the moment, we believe our assumptions or beliefs are true, and that is why they are so painful. Distorted assumptions or beliefs create the suffering of trauma.

Shattered Dreams by Larry Crabb was very insightful for me as I was working my way through betrayal. In the beginning, it seemed like all my dreams about marriage, family, and my future were shattered. I was not even sure who I was married to anymore. When we were married, Mark was going to seminary, and I was fully on board to follow him and that vision. All my dreams were shattered when his secret life was exposed fifteen years later. The thoughts in *Shattered Dreams* placed my pain in a larger context, however. Rather than seeking the happiness that often comes from quick solutions or rushed fixes to get out of pain, I needed to consider that God was working on creating long-term joy in my life that comes from getting to know him, trust him, and depend on him more in my wounded place.[13]

Purpose in Your Pain

Is it true that all trials can lead to transformation? Will God really use our pain for something good? Is it true he will not waste our pain? Can it be used to grow us up spiritually?

Scripture continually reminds us that pain was meant to help us, heal us, and transform us. God does not want us to be a victim of our pain and shattered dreams. Victims spread their pain all over other people by spewing unhealthy emotions through anger, rage, blame, and out-of-control behavior. Or they ingest their pain and carry around emotions inside their bodies that play havoc on their physical and mental well-being. Either way, a victim of pain does not live with joy and peace—God's greatest gifts to us on earth.

We can learn a lot about ourselves when we live through pain. Many clients have asked me, "How can I get through this betrayal?" We all ask that question when we are in pain. If you are hurting, I hope this book will help you with practical ways to *slowly* transform the wounds in your body, heart, and mind. While I am a counselor, one who is often looked to for answers and advice, I tell my clients that I believe God has gifted each of us with the Holy Spirit. I liken the Spirit's work to the GPS equipment we use to direct us to places, except in this case it is God's Positioning System—that voice or nudge to go in a certain direction. And when we have missed his mark, he disturbs our peace until we make another turn. It is an amazing system. He will direct our paths as we learn to listen to that still, quiet voice of his Spirit within.

I want this book to help you connect to the Holy Spirit's lead for determining your next right step to well-being—to getting through hard stuff and becoming "mature and complete, not lacking anything" as you do so. I will join you on the journey and be your companion. That is my role as a counselor too.

▶ Turn to the Gentle Assignments section on page 171 for further reflection.

2

Getting Practical
When You Are in Pain

Our glory is hidden in our pain, if we allow God to bring the gift
of himself in our experience of it. If we turn to God, not rebelling
against our hurt, we let God transform it into greater good. We
let others join us and discover it with us.

Henri Nouwen

WHAT CAN YOU DO IN THE FACE OF PAIN that follows adversity? This chapter introduces you to small, practical steps you can take to ease your agony. You may be experiencing relational trauma such as a divorce, you or a loved one may be bearing an illness, or maybe you have been in an accident. Maybe you are dealing with the consequences of the pandemic; in my case, I am suffering the loss of my husband. Or your pain may be from an accumulation of these or other traumatic life experiences.

It may seem like there are too many next steps to focus on here. Let me encourage you to start slowly. Choose one of the ideas to focus on first. When you think you have made some progress in one area, move on and choose another. It may be that you quickly read through this whole book to get an overview of growing through traumatic experiences, and then return to work more specifically on some of these suggestions. There is no one right way. The process takes time. Becoming your best self is not a sprint, it is a marathon.

I have experienced that these steps lead to thriving, being more authentic, and eventually growing to become the person God created me to be. Please be gentle with yourself. This work is not easy or fast. So let me say it again: please be patient and kind to yourself as you try some of these ideas. Anything new will seem awkward at first.

Start with the Basics

Pain has a way of distracting you from the things you need to function well: good sleep, good food, good exercise, and sufficient money. So, begin with the basics. Traumatic events in your life send your thoughts in a myriad of directions. When your thoughts are replaying and swirling, you are probably not sleeping. Some folks keep pushing through, saying it is not that bad. Or they become a victim and say there is nothing they can do but endure it. If you want to work on emotional well-being, you must prioritize sleep. Call your doctor or visit an integrative professional and be honest. You cannot be your best when you are sleep deprived. You cannot think well, you are short on patience, you are irritable, you are reactive. You are not good to others, and you probably start disliking yourself as well.

Many people find it difficult to eat well when they face adversity. Some turn to comfort food to manage difficult times, eating gobs of simple carbohydrates or sugar and drinking caffeine or alcohol to cope with unwanted emotions. It is understandable. These give you a quick burst of energy or sense of calm. In the long run, though, you can become addicted to unhealthy foods that deplete your brain health and physical well-being. Be conscious about substituting some healthy choices into your daily meals. You do not need to be perfect. But each time you make a healthier choice for your body, you choose yourself. Each time you choose yourself, you begin to love yourself more too.

It is difficult to want to move and exercise when life strikes you down. We have all experienced that. When trials trip you up, the last things you feel like doing are the things that would be better for you. I do not know why this happens, and I have certainly battled this tendency. Asking someone to regularly encourage you to get out and walk, work in the garden, or go on a bike ride might help you get started. Accountability means having others help you follow through on your good intentions when you do not feel like it. It is about loving encouragement.

Another essential component to your emotional well-being is having enough money to take care of your basic needs. When your life has fractured, sometimes you simply do not know whether you have money or not. Perhaps your spouse controlled all the finances and has threatened to withhold money during this time. Perhaps you have never taken an interest in learning about your financial situation and now depend on what you are given. Whatever the case, it is important for you to get help to determine what you have access to, in order to care for yourself and anyone else who depends on you, such as children. You may need a good friend who understands financial matters, an accountant, a financial planner, or an attorney to help sort things out. The fear that grows for those who do not know if they are financially stable is paralyzing. It gets in the way of making wise decisions and keeps them victimized by their situation. Things do not need to be that way.

Making healthy choices about sleep, food, exercise, and money are simple ways to begin pouring back into yourself. When you choose yourself, you invest in yourself and start loving yourself more.

Slow Down

One of the immediate side effects of being in pain, whether physical or emotional, is that it slows your life down. We have all become experts at multitasking and speeding life up so that we can fit more in. We are hurried people. We like fast everything—fast information, fast food, fast service, fast results. The problem with fast is that it causes you to miss connecting with what you are feeling and thinking, and you begin to live in reaction to life. You function on autopilot rather than intentionally deciding what you will do.

So, what is so necessary about slowing down? One benefit is the ability it gives you to observe more carefully. That is a trait of anyone who wants to learn something. When Mark and I traveled to Europe on our honeymoon almost fifty years ago, we decided to take the Silver Bullet train from England to Scotland. I was excited to settle into my comfy seat on the train and take in the beautiful countryside. To my surprise, the Silver Bullet lived up to its name by going two hundred miles an hour. I could not focus on anything out the window as it was whizzing by, and I had to hide my eyes in a book for fear of getting motion sickness. I was so disappointed. The train went too fast for me to experience anything in that gorgeous country. It taught me a lot about slowing down, however, and the memory has been a good reminder that if I want to observe something, I need to slow down.

Slowing down can teach you some new things about yourself if you will let it. We tend to fight the slowing down process. Try inviting it in and see where it takes you. Many women I counsel have reported that they have withdrawn from commitments and committees, from gatherings and traditions, from extravagant entertainment and complicated meals. They pared down to a simpler life when they were in a lot of pain. And they discovered that life went on. Nothing horrible happened. Others could step up when they stepped out. That can be a good life lesson: *I am not indispensable. I do not need to do it all. Others will help.*

Find Companionship

We need each other. You do not need just anyone; you need people who can be safe for you when you are living through a season of adversity. One of the greatest components to managing crisis and trauma is finding people who can journey with you. You do not need to be alone. A counselor is trained to be safe and can encourage you to share without judgment or advice, and hopefully without overspiritualizing. If your counselor does not create a safe environment, then try another. You will know when you have experienced a safe counseling session. You will feel better leaving than when you came. The same is true when you are with other safe people. They will not tell you what you should do or why this is going to be good for you. You will not be peppered with questions, criticized, or judged. They will not become more emotional about your pain than you are. A safe person listens carefully and offers support in whatever way you ask for it. That might be sitting still with you in silence. Nothing more.

You do not need to be alone. There are safe people who have experienced what you are going through, or something similar. These people lighten your pain—they give you hope, a helping hand, and a reminder that you are not crazy.

Invest in Yourself

Many Christians have focused on loving others and caring for their needs to the exclusion of caring for themselves. They have given and given and given until they cannot squeeze out one more ounce of energy for anything. Sarah Young, in *Jesus Calling*, calls this "drainout—countless interactions with needy people."[1] Those who do so are depleted and disconnected from their own needs. They are irritable and depressed.

Learning how to take care of yourself is essential for anyone choosing to be well, and especially so if you are in pain. Trauma of any kind can exhaust your body and your emotions. If you do not learn to be kind to yourself, you may stay emotionally and physically depleted for a long time. You may notice other people trying to take care of you because they perceive that you are not doing enough for yourself. Some of you may like that feeling. It can feel like being loved. However, if most of your self-care is coming from others or the suggestions of others, this will not create well-being for you in the long term. You must learn to choose yourself and to know what you need to feel physically and emotionally filled up. When you are filled, you will be available to give to others.

Learning to care for yourself can be a challenge if you have not been encouraged or taught to attend to your needs. Some of you may have heard that a Christian's job is to attend to others. Period. Or maybe you have watched a parent who was totally self-less, and that was held up as a wonderful character trait. Maybe your needs have been ignored or minimized. Whatever the beliefs that you carry from others, Scripture says that you are a temple of God. You need to care for yourself because you do not want your temple to fall into disrepair.

Create a POYO

Quite a while ago, I was reading a book entitled *The Not So Big House* by Sarah Susanka. Sarah is a Minneapolis architect who helps folks find beauty and well-being in smaller spaces, not larger ones. I was immediately struck by an acronym she uses: POYO, or a Place of Your Own.[2] She believes everyone needs a space to call their own, where they can hang out, store their private things, rejuvenate, shed some tears, or call a friend. It can be for personal reflection and relaxation. It can be for creativity and vision. It can be for grieving and connecting with God. It can be for whatever you need it to be.

I loved that idea, and I have practiced it for myself. I realized that I had always shared spaces with someone: first with my twin sister, where our bedroom was forever a compromise of what she wanted and what I wanted, then with college roommates, and soon after college graduation I married Mark and shared all my spaces with him. I never had a POYO!

I have been very intentional about creating a POYO; in fact, I have been kidded about the fact that I have found a way to create several POYOs in the bedroom spaces vacated by our grown children. One allows me to sink into my devotional time uninterrupted, another offers the perfectly calm, organized workspace that I love for business, and yet another breathes creativity into my writing. A POYO is a treat to your soul. You need one! Figure out where you can carve out a spot of your own. It could be a corner in a storage room, a cleared-out closet, a chair downstairs in the laundry room, a guest room, an unused space under the staircase—almost anywhere. It just needs to be *your* space where you can put whatever you value, and it will not be used or disrupted by anyone else. In fact, a POYO is a private place that needs an invitation to enter.

Have some fun exploring where you will land. Get creative. Buy a new lamp or a new chair. Try a basket to hold your journal and books. Art pieces may add meaning to your vision, or a soft blanket may bring comfort when you are sad. Bring things into your POYO that represent you. This place is where you will take time for yourself, which for many of you is not something you are familiar with. It is a place where others will respect your privacy, which may also be lacking in your busy life. I think you are going to like it. If you have a family, I think you will find that your spouse and kids would enjoy a POYO too.

Explore the Concept of Both/And

I use *and* a lot when I speak and write. In a sentence, the word asks you to pay attention to the parts on either side of it, because both parts are true. It means that what is going to be said is complicated and is not black-and-white. The truth is usually not simple, and enduring painful life experiences is complicated. The truth usually compels us to hold the tension of two ideas, feelings, or behaviors at once. It does not ask us to eliminate part of what is true.

Jim Collins has written two powerful books for people in business based on his extensive research on what makes some businesses thrive while others do not. In *Built to Last*, he writes about the "Tyranny of the OR" and the "Genius of the AND." He says companies oppress themselves with the Tyranny of the OR and cannot accept the paradox of two seemingly contradictory forces or ideas at the same time. People must believe in either A or B, but not both. Examples might be, "You can have change *or* stability," "You can be conservative *or* bold," "You can have low cost *or* high quality." Highly visionary companies, however, embrace the Genius of the AND, says Collins. They figure out a way to have both A *and* B![3]

That is what I desire for myself and for you—a highly visionary life that can embrace the complexity of pain *and* growth.

Notice how using *and* rather than *but* begins to change the meaning of what is said. When we use *but* in our sentences, it negates the first part of what we said. We only keep half of the sentence for our truth. *And* allows us to embrace the tension of holding two or more ideas, emotions, or behaviors at one time.

This *and* has the power to begin change in your life. Begin trying it yourself. Most women I counsel admit they are black-and-white thinkers. Always or never. Good or bad. Right or wrong. This way or that way. Notice how you feel when you start to use this new *and* way of thinking and speaking. It is freeing because it is truthful. It will allow you to live in the complexity of life.

Here are a few examples:

- I love writing, *and* it takes a lot of time and energy that I sometimes do not have.
- I do not like to be in pain, *and* I have learned that God is teaching me something in it.

- The COVID pandemic has limited many of my normal activities, *and* I have learned to appreciate some simpler ways of living.
- I have many loving people around me, *and* I still feel lonely at times.
- I wish Mark was still here with me, *and* I am glad he is not in pain anymore.

Remember the Slinky and the Roller Coaster

When people seek help, they often expect their emotions to level off and their progress to be consistent. Unfortunately, the reality usually appears quite differently. The Slinky is a wonderful metaphor for how progress often looks. Slinkies move forward by creating an up and down movement, edging forward ever so craftily. It is only both the upward swing and the lower dip that allow this miraculous forward propulsion. At our counseling center, this is exactly what clients experience as they move through their emotions from a traumatic event. There is progress and then, seemingly, backsliding. If you are not careful, you may start believing you have lost momentum, you are back to the beginning—you are failing. Your Slinky progress, though, is just as it should be: some emotional ups followed by some emotional downs, all working together to move you forward!

One of the ways you may have been able to control your emotions and keep them contained was to find behaviors or substances to block them or shut them down. If you are working on being authentic and honest about how you are feeling, all your emotions will start showing up more regularly, in whatever way they want to express themselves. If you are working on eliminating ways you have blocked them, then they could start looking like a roller coaster. Up and down and round and round, those feelings are going to be all over the place. You can feel like you are going backward in growing through pain. Some people believe they are doing well if their emotions are in check. Truthfully, though, it may be that you are becoming more authentic and real when your emotions are messy. You may also be making up for a lot of time spent suppressing those feelings and not allowing them to be expressed. Looking like you are on a roller coaster with your emotions for a while can be a sign of progress.

Learn to Grieve Well

All change creates loss, and all loss creates painful feelings. Even when you choose to make a change—like moving to a new house, taking a new job, having a baby—it still creates loss and thus many emotions. You leave a house behind with many memories of the years you lived there. There is loss. You leave a familiar job and friends you have worked with for a time. There is loss. You have a new baby, and you sacrifice time for yourself. And there is loss. Grieving is moving through loss. It is an important process that allows you to clear out the emotions that accumulate from loss so that you can allow your heart to move on to future living.

Even the word *emotion* in Latin means "to move through." Trying to "forget it and move on" rarely works. Releasing emotions caused by the loss is necessary work to move through something painful. You probably have experienced how relieving it is to have a good cry. It is also tiring. Perhaps when Solomon writes, "A sad face is good for the heart" (Eccles. 7:3), he is suggesting that sorrow and suffering lead to great opportunities once the heart can be heard.

In ancient times, people would gather to pray at a wailing wall. It was a place of comfort and consolation in misfortune. In *The Secret Life of Bees*, two of the three Boatwright sisters decided to build a wailing wall for May, their sister who bore much sadness after the loss of her twin sister. They gathered stones from a nearby river and piled them atop one another to create a wailing wall. When May visited this stone wall, she wrote down the names of people in pain or events that caused her pain and put the notes in

the wall.[4] It was her POYO where she could release her accumulated pain. She was able to leave some of her suffering at the wall.
Having a safe place to go to focus on mourning a loss is healing.
It eventually helps you move through the normal stages of grief,
which include emotions such as shock and numbness, anger and
confusion, sadness and acceptance. Your POYO can be one of
those safe places. My car is one of mine. Driving offers me the
opportunity to be totally silent, which allows my heart to think
and feel whatever it needs to . . . sometimes for hours at a time. I
have most recently realized that visiting Mark's gravesite is another
holy place to grieve.

Where do you think your wailing wall could be? If you find
a consistent place to sit and pray and "let your face be sad," it
becomes a holy place. Sitting in that same place takes you to your
emotional grieving. It is as if your body knows the work it is called
to do, and it readily releases the emotions that are flooding your
heart. As Psalm 126:5 says, "Those who sow with tears will reap
with songs of joy." Our tears can be seeds that will grow into a
harvest of joy because God is able to bring good out of tragedy.
Your heart heals when your heart feels.

Grieving often cries out for other safe people to be fair witnesses
of our pain. You will benefit by taking a vulnerable step to include
them in your process. I do not know why our emoting is validated
by the presence of loved ones, *and* I know it is. These witnesses
must be people who are not advising you or prodding you to get
on to something. They are there to let you share. Period.

Let's pause here. Adversity has crushed your routines, relationships, safety, or sense of direction. When you feel anxious because
a big chunk of future needs to be figured out, stop and think
about a *next right step*. We have explored several first steps to
move through adversity and trauma: caring for your basic needs,
finding safe people you can talk to, creating a POYO, broadening

your black-and-white beliefs to *and* thoughts, and allowing your-self to grieve your losses well, knowing your progress will have ups and downs.

These small next right steps may appear as if they are not doing anything to resolve a complex, difficult situation. Our natural inclination is to figure things out, have an agenda, plan, execute, and create change. Taking small steps to focus on being present to your pain and to decide what is needed in this moment or day could be foreign to you. It can also be the start of walking through your pain and depending on God, not just yourself, for answers. Eventually, you will walk into a future that looks quite different. God will not waste your pain.

▶ Turn to the Gentle Assignments section on page 171 for further reflection.

3

Surviving or Thriving

To fashion an inner story of our pain carries us into the heart of
it, which is where rebirth inevitably occurs.

Sue Monk Kidd

CAN PAIN LEAD TO A BETTER LIFE? Or do we just get better at
hanging on, getting from one day to the next, putting up walls to
keep pain away? Our earthly bodies and brains have been created
with automatic responses to danger. We call this the *sympathetic
nervous system*. It helps us survive. Thank God we have this, because we often need to respond hurriedly, such as to reckless driving, a dog ready to attack, a burglar entering our home, a gash in
our skin that is bleeding profusely, or a person who is hurting us.

Surviving adversity is about responding quickly to dangerous
situations. It is an automatic response from our built-in systems.
We will fight, flee, or freeze when we are in danger. Which is your
automatic response when you feel danger? Being able to observe
and name this is a first step to potentially changing your reaction.
Your automatic response may be helpful to survive, but it may

also hinder your ability to thrive. Surviving is about staying alive. Thriving is about loving your life.

Why would you want something more than surviving? Isn't that goal enough? Why do you need to ask if your painful experience would help you grow? Can pain lead to something better?

I love sports because they give us so many stories of successful athletes who have overcome obstacles. Athletes describe their comebacks from setbacks and their perseverance through injuries. I once heard an interview with a professional golfer at a tournament, and he said that when he and his wife almost lost their baby, his whole perspective about his career changed. Golf was no longer the focus of his life. When my son was ten years old and did a lot of bench-sitting for the basketball team he played on, one day an accomplished former pro player approached him after a game. He acknowledged to my son that it was hard not to be in the game, *and* he'd learned the most during a year when he'd sat the bench himself.

The stories of people in communities that have overcome natural disasters offer the same encouragement. We see the wreckage on our news stations, and we wonder how people survive. Yet they do. When reporters interview folks from these sites of devastation, we often hear gratitude for what they still have—each other—and not only grief over what was lost.

We have all been experiencing a pandemic that has caused financial and physical loss all around us. We do not know how it will all turn out. I trust that there has been and will continue to be thriving amid these losses as well. As communities have returned to more normal interactions, people are sharing the positive changes they've experienced. Life slowed down and people spent more time with family. We enjoyed simpler activities and companies got more resourceful. We found creative ways of using our resources and talents to support each other. In time, the trials and pain that came from numerous limitations produced change and growth.

There are also books that suggest there is more for us than surviving life. *What Doesn't Kill Us* by Stephen Joseph, *Turn My*

Mourning into Dancing by Henri Nouwen, *Rising Strong* by Brené Brown, *Trauma and Transformation* by Tedeschi and Calhoun, the Bible—I could fill many pages here with articles and books that tell you life is hard *and* there is growth available through the hardship. We root for the underdog. It is easy to cheer on the overcomers. Maybe in their stories we catch a glimpse that we could be like them: someone who knows how to come from behind, knows how to overcome obstacles, knows that in everything we can learn something. These stories teach us we can be better, not bitter, from trials. I am confident God wants that for us. He does not want any of us to be victims, to just hang on.

Remember Thriving Is Spiritual Growth

I believe we are all wired for spiritual growth. Do any of us want to settle for a life of survival? Surviving is about defending yourself from others and the world. Your sole focus is you and how to protect and comfort yourself when you are hurt. You have no song in your heart, no spark or joy. God wants something better for you. He has given you a desire to become more Christlike in character. He created you with passion and purpose to use your talents to serve him. It is a far richer life that will involve being intentional and proactive. It involves getting closer to people. That can be difficult because when you get closer, you are more vulnerable and can get hurt more easily. How can you get closer *and* still take good care of yourself? How can you love others *and* love yourself? That is the challenge and the reward of thriving.

We all hate pain, and sometimes figuring out how to survive is the quickest way to relieve it. Surviving allows us to manage the moment, which can be good for a while. Yet surviving may involve behaviors or substances that are not good for you or your relationships and can create isolation or push others away. You may not really like who you are when you are surviving. Generally, others do not find you very likable when you are surviving, either.

What if God wanted to use your pain for some greater purpose? What if something traumatic could be transformational? What if you could be counted among the overcomers James writes about?

Consider it pure joy, my brothers and sisters, whenever you face trials of many kinds, because you know that the testing of your faith produces perseverance. Let perseverance finish its work so that you may be mature and complete, not lacking anything. (James 1:2–4)

James is not talking about surviving here. He is talking about prevailing, about experiencing something *greater* than what was before the trial. Today we call that posttraumatic growth: the positive life changes experienced as a result of struggling with a highly stressful life experience. This growth process transforms something traumatic into something good. It reminds me of the phenomenon called *upcycling*. You take something old and worn-out and make it into something new, and it becomes even more valuable.

God wants to mature us in our Christian walk. He wants to make us more Christlike and valuable to others. He wants us to find the deeper joy of depending on him to be there for all our needs. Pastor Rick Warren says, "We learn things about God in suffering that we can't learn any other way."[1]

Could you be open to the idea that something traumatic in your life could lead to thriving? Some of you may be saying, "My life was really good, and I *was* thriving—until I learned about my husband's infidelity. And now I am not. He is clearly the reason why I am miserable and unable to thrive anymore." Yes, that makes sense, *and* it could be there is even more thriving available to you once you move through this latest trial. There could be even more relational and character growth that God wants for you. Could you be open to that possibility?

▶ Turn to the Gentle Assignments section on page 173 for further reflection.

4

Practical Steps to Move from Surviving to Thriving

In the midst of winter I found that there was, in me, an invincible summer.

Albert Camus

GOD WANTS TO MATURE YOU in your Christian walk. Let's explore together some practical things he may be up to when you are first confronted with a crisis. These next right steps do not solve the whole situation immediately but are suggestions that may help you live in the present and practice a new way to live when life is hard. They are not about looking forward weeks or months into the future. They are not about trying to change or control someone else to find more peace in your life. They are meant to help you change things about yourself so that, slowly, you can see yourself becoming someone quite different from who you were before the crisis.

Let's dive in. You may want to move quickly by and read more of the book before deciding to settle down and do any assignments. That's fine. Choose what feels right for you.

Take Responsibility for Yourself

Deciding you will take responsibility for your decisions and behaviors means you will not blame others when you are not happy, safe, fulfilled, rested, productive, respected, loved, valued, or anything else that is important to you. It means you will not justify your unhealthy behaviors because someone else did not meet your need or was acting unhealthily. Things happen in life to temporarily rock you from these places of thriving, *and*, ultimately, you have choices to change things. You may try to change another person through criticizing, nagging, demanding, or controlling, but these efforts do not work. This is not to say you cannot ask for your needs to be met. If others are not willing to cooperate, you can take responsibility to *do* something for yourself. You can change yourself. Trying to change another person to make your life better does not work.

Taking responsibility for yourself is not an easy challenge. It totally shifts how you look at your life. Instead of wishing for others to live like you want them to so you will be happy, loved, valued, and fulfilled, you take charge of creating the life you want.

Taking responsibility for your life and happiness is the first step in deciding you want to get well when you have been leveled by life. God will do amazing things when you sign up for this journey. He wants you to work at this precious life he has given you. And he will be with you always as you do so.

Live Authentically

Being authentic, or *congruent*, means that your inside emotions, thoughts, and needs match your outside words and behaviors.

They go together. People who are not authentic can confuse or hurt you. Those who lie to you are not authentic. Those who tell you they are "fine" when they are not fine are confusing. They are not being congruent. Have you heard of the old recovery definition of FINE? Finicky, Insecure, Neurotic, and Emotional. It is possible that people who are going around telling everyone they are fine all the time have a lot more going on!

Living congruently builds trust. Others can depend on you because you are not different in different situations or with different people. You are not different in private places than in public places. It is peaceful to live congruently. Does being congruent sound appealing to you? Authenticity will lead to you being *you* with your personality, your talents, your strengths, your weaknesses, your needs, your contentment, and your joy. It will lead to thriving. Since you are working on what you can change, I suggest that you work on *your* authenticity, regardless of what someone else might choose to do.

See Your Feelings As Messengers

Feelings are messengers from your soul. They are important because they will inform you of things you need. They have purpose. They will let you know a lot of things about yourself if you invite them to. So many people are afraid of emotions. If God did not intend for emotions to be helpful to you, he would have made your body incapable of expressing them.

Jesus allows his many emotions to be known in Scripture. One poignant story describes Mary and Martha desperately sending word to Jesus to help Lazarus, their brother, who was very ill. Jesus stayed two extra days before going to his friends' house, where Lazarus had already died. When he saw Mary's anguish, Scripture says, "[Jesus] was deeply moved in spirit and troubled. . . . Jesus wept" (John 11:33–35). When you read the entire story, you hear Jesus's compassion, sorrow, and even frustration as he

49

tries to explain why he allowed Lazarus to die a human death before raising him to life again. Jesus knows all the emotions people experience. He experienced them also.

What are you feeling? That is a simple question most people do not know how to answer, at least with feeling words other than *good*, *fine*, or *tired*. And some would add *mad*. When life slows down in crisis, you have the opportunity to observe, *What am I feeling?*

Many of us are uncomfortable or incapable of talking about our feelings. We would rather talk about work, kids, accomplishments, plans, vacations, people we know—anything other than vulnerable heart conversation. Many of us have learned not to trust our feelings. You may believe feelings lead you astray, and you must make wise decisions only from your thoughts or from the wisdom of other people. Parents may not talk about feelings because it was not modeled for them by their parents. It can be easier to tell children what to do than to figure out what feelings are trying to "say."

Feelings are a first step to being authentic. When you talk about what you are feeling, you are taking a first step to being congruent. Turn to appendix A for a chart of some words to describe your feelings. This is not an exhaustive list, *and* it can get you started thinking about more words to expand your emotional vocabulary.

When Mark's addiction was discovered, I tried hard to look "normal" and not let others see my pain. I was a master of deception in public. In the privacy of my home, however, my feelings spilled out profusely. I learned that, to be authentic, there are more than two choices about sharing. Sharing everything or sharing nothing is black-and-white thinking. There are many more choices that help you feel congruent. I could have shared that my life was hard right then, or I was feeling sad, or I was sorting out some things with the help of a counselor. Depending upon who I was talking to and how close that relationship was, I had many choices of what would be congruent for me to say other than "I'm fine."

Why is it healthy to work on being congruent about your feelings with others? First, it is good for *you* to speak your truth aloud so that you hear and understand yourself. Sometimes, in counseling, we use words like "Your little one inside is hurting and wants to know that adult you listens and understands her." For some of you, this may sound very foreign. If you can, imagine that today, as an adult, you can provide for and protect your "little one"—your heart—from hurt and danger and beliefs that are not true. Most of you probably longed for more of that in your life when you were young. Now you can be that adult for yourself.

Second, being congruent in your conversations will start to be more natural over time, and you will not have to think about it so much. Your authenticity will come more fluently. You will feel more peaceful. Others will know you as you are and will feel safer with you. Remember, being authentic builds trust with others. People do not have to figure you out, which is tiring and often inaccurate. Being truthful is a great gift to building relationships.

Every feeling carries with it a need. If you are sad, you may need time alone. If you are scared, you may need someone to be with you. If you are exhausted, you may need a nap. If you are frustrated, you may need more information. If you are angry and irritable, you may need a break from your work. Every feeling is a messenger for something you need.

You may soon learn that feelings are complicated, just like other truths in life, and several words could describe your feelings at any given time. These can even be opposites! You can feel content *and* sad, a little hopeful *and* yet hopeless, irritated *and* calm. Understanding how complex your emotions are is enlightening. Hopefully, it helps you accept why your emotions feel overwhelming at times. It is all right to have all of them, because that is what is authentic.

Ask Yourself: How Do I Cope?

If you do not know how to describe what you are feeling, you may miss the chance of knowing what you need. Instead, you may just find a way to manage that feeling, or as we say at our counseling center, you find a way to *cope*. Coping refers to ways we avoid certain uncomfortable feelings. These are not particularly healthy choices, either. When you use certain behaviors or substances to cope, you generally feel worse after the fact. And your legitimate need has not been attended to. Coping helps you survive. It does not help you thrive.

Let's explore what coping is and see if you can identify some of the things you do or substances you use to cope. You can do this by being an observer. There is no judgment. There is no pressure to change anything—yet. Once you name some of your coping strategies, you can decide if you want to change anything as you move toward thriving. The behaviors or substances you are engaging in to avoid certain difficult feelings are not necessarily awful, hurtful choices, *and* they pull you away from being your authentic self and from building healthy relationships. You usually do not look very pretty when you are coping. No one does. Sometimes coping choices are sinful and damaging to you and your relationships. In all cases, they do not contribute to a life of thriving.

You may use some of the same behaviors or substances at another time and they give you energy and "life." They are positively influencing your well-being. In that case I would identify them as *self-care*. You are feeding your soul, you are being congruent, and you are loving yourself well.

Here is a list of some behaviors/substances people may use to cope with difficult emotions. Ask yourself, *When I get mad, sad, scared, lonely, or ashamed, what do I tend to do?* Circle the ones that apply to you. Then put squares around the ones you have used since you were a young child. This is not an exhaustive list, so add others that apply to you.

Withdrawing	Video games
Alcohol	Social media
Illegal drugs	Work
Emotional eating	Overparenting
Sleeping	Lying
Raging	Gambling
Blaming others	Gardening
Excessive exercise	Chocolate
Reading	Excessive caregiving
Hobbies	Self-righteousness
TV	Socializing
Addictions	Church activities
Romance novels	Pornography
Unhealthy sex	Movies
Facebook	Affairs
Sarcasm	Shopping
Volunteering	Sex
Sports	Traveling

This list contains some behaviors and substances that can be used to give you energy and life. Remember, what is important to consider is your *motivation* for choosing it. "When I am lonely, I find comfort food." "When I am angry, I get sarcastic." "When I need to feel valued, I volunteer a lot." "When I want to avoid difficult situations with the kids, I go to work." You may have used one of these without much thought. It's familiar, a habit learned a long time ago. The ones you put a square around become some of the hardest to change because they have been part of your life for so long. Lying is a good example of that. When people have betrayed spouses sexually or emotionally, lying accompanies that betrayal. For most people, stopping their lying or not telling the whole truth is far more difficult to do than stopping the betrayal behaviors. Lying as a coping behavior usually starts early in life. For me, I became a "good girl" to avoid pain. If I were good enough, I reasoned, I would be free of pain. I would not get into trouble. I also got busy doing things. That included work. I knew how to withdraw and be quiet. All those things helped me avoid dealing with painful situations or conflict. It is true that sometimes these choices can be healthy and serve to energize me. In those cases, I call it self-care. But when they are used to avoid or minimize difficult emotions or circumstances, then I call it unhealthy coping.

Let's review the difference of unhealthy coping versus self-care one more time. Unhealthy coping choices pull you away from others. You survive on your own. The goal is to comfort yourself or to protect yourself. Self-care choices lead to thriving. You feel energized, relieved, and peaceful when you choose self-care. There is a huge difference in how you live and the joy you feel. You have a choice.

Identify and Communicate Your Needs

A big sigh. Rolled eyes. Irritable responses. Long silences. Blaming others. These and other passive ways of living with others are our unhealthy attempts to get needs met. We call them *passive* because they do not directly tell another person what we need. Life would be much easier if we were all good at stating our needs and desires. Most often, we do not get a clear message of what someone wants.

When you receive passive messages, you then have to try to figure out what that person needs, because passive messages are indirect. You sense something is needed, but you do not know what. You may then feel anxious, which leads you to problem-solve for another person or to ask a lot of questions. Do you find yourself doing these things?

Many people seem to live by this belief: "If you really love me, you should know what I need!" This mindset kills a relationship, because humans are not mind readers. I will say it again: we do not have the ability to read the minds of others. Reading someone's mind so that we automatically know what they need is not a necessary sign to prove we love them. What I do know is that people get irritated when others try to solve problems for them or give advice, unless they are invited to give that kind of help. The pattern that emerges when someone tries to uncover your unexpressed needs—whether by trying to read your mind or by trying to be helpful when you have not asked—feels like that of a parent talking to a child. It is a no-win pattern for adult relationships. No adult wants to feel like a child. If you are an adult in a relationship, it is your job to figure out your needs and to clearly communicate them. It is that simple. Only, I know it is not.

Women I work with find it difficult to change this part of who they are. In other words, they have difficulty stating their needs and asking for help. Most of them are very independent and capable people. For one reason or another, they have learned how to manage things alone. Perhaps one of their parents was not available due to work, health issues, or divorce, and they stepped in to take care of adult responsibilities. Maybe they grew up in a large family and, as an older sibling, they were given responsibilities to care for younger ones. It may have been a value in the family to take care of things themselves and not ask for help. Many women would tell you they have taken care of more than their share in relationships or their family for a long time; they are very responsible. They are not accustomed to asking others for their needs. Sometimes they have asked for but have not received any help. Out of frustration, they take care of things alone. This is not always a negative choice, *and* it can leave them exhausted and living like martyrs.

Identifying your needs and desires and asking others to help you at times is a component of being emotionally healthy. If you never need others, you miss the chance to tell someone, "You are important to me. I have chosen you to be with me in this need." When a neighbor says, "I cannot get these plants to grow, and

I was thinking maybe you could help me," aren't you grateful for that chance to help? When a friend calls and asks "Can you have coffee with me? I have something I need to talk over with a trusted person," do you not feel blessed by her asking? When you surrender your need to do it all by yourself all the time and ask for help meeting your needs, you include others in your life. That can feel wonderful—and it can grow your relationships. It will also unburden you from the belief that you have to do life all alone.

I have a few questions for you:

- Do you stop and eat when your body is hungry?
- Do you allow yourself to go to bed instead of pushing yourself to finish your to-do list?
- Do you ask for help when you feel overwhelmed or too tired?
- Do you exercise regularly?
- Do you feel responsible for other people's well-being? Children? Spouse? Parents?
- Do you take time away from your children? Your spouse?
- Do you have a few people to call and talk to when you are hurting?
- Do you spend money on yourself sometimes, just for fun?
- Do you know what kind of food you like if someone asks you to go out to eat?
- Do you take time to have fun?
- Do you have hobbies?
- Can you allow your house or yourself to be messy sometimes?
- Do you take time to read or learn something new?
- Do you find yourself sacrificing most of the time because there is not enough time or money for you?

Do you struggle to know what you need and to ask for help, creating a life *independent* from others? Do you have so many needs and desires that you are too *dependent* on others to help you out? There is a balance in there somewhere that will feel good and healthy for you. If you want to thrive, you will learn how to take care of yourself when you need to *and* know you can ask for help too.

What were you taught about having needs and asking for help when you were younger? You may have learned that you should not have needs—your main job is to take care of others' needs. You may have learned that it is selfish to have needs. You may have learned that no one is trustworthy and that you had better take care of all your needs by yourself. You may have learned that your spouse's needs are more important than yours. Or that you should always attend to your children's needs first. Different people have either spoken these rules to you, or you have watched them play out in other significant people in your life. Whatever you learned in the past, you have the power to decide what you believe today about having needs and expressing them.

As you think about your needs or desires and talk about them, you will find you have more peace and joy in your days. When you get used to naming your needs and asking for help when you are overwhelmed, your life will run smoother and more joyfully. You will love it! And others will like being around you more too.

Explore Your Motivation

Asking myself *What is my motivation?* helps me fine-tune my decisions. If my motivation is not coming from my needs or is not "on the mark" with what God wants for me, then things do not work out so well.

If you asked your spouse to leave when he hurt you, was it because *you needed him* to experience some consequence or because *you* needed time and space away from him? When your motivation comes from a need of your own—you need time alone when you are hurting—you will likely find your decision feels more authentic and you feel more peaceful. If you are trying to change someone else or teach them a lesson, that motivation is not healthy for you. The first is about self-care and loving yourself. The second is about controlling another person. Controlling never works. It only creates ongoing conflict about who is going to be more powerful and in control. There is no peace that comes from trying to control others. As the twelve-step programs say, "You can only change yourself." Start there.

Live Intentionally

The difference between surviving and thriving is a matter of reacting to life versus being intentional about it. When you react to life, you wait for things to happen and then respond. And you usually respond hurriedly and without much thought, from that autopilot place within your brain. Reactive living will lead you to some of those behaviors or substances on the coping list. It is what you usually do. It is what you cannot help but do. You react in a typical fashion, often an old pattern established in earlier life. Paul said it perfectly in Romans 7:15: "I do not understand what I do. For what I want to do I do not do, but what I hate I do."

Thankfully, the brain is *malleable*, which means it can change. Practicing new responses can rewire the brain to respond differently. You can override some of the old ways you have automatically responded to pain and fear. It takes practice, and some therapies such as EMDR (eye movement desensitization and reprocessing), neurofeedback, or equine therapy can help.

Let's look at a few examples of reactionary living:

If a child or spouse yells at you, you might yell in return.
If you do not feel cared for, you may shut down and not talk to that person.

If you have been relationally betrayed, you may try harder to be more sexual.

If you have been hurt, you may find a way to get revenge.

If you feel lonely, you may reach for another glass of wine.

If you feel scared, you might eat some comforting, unhealthy foods.

Living life reactively can at times be good, especially when you need a quick response to a dangerous situation. When a child runs out into the street, you react quickly. When you touch a hot grill, you immediately pull away. When someone is hitting you, you hopefully run away or quickly fight back. Remember, not all reactionary behaviors are unwanted. There are times when being reactionary is good, *and* there are times when quick responses are not consistent with your well-being.

A reactionary life means being a victim and not becoming the person you want to be. There is always someone or something that gets in the way of your life being better—and of you being the best version of yourself. You forget that you have choices and can work to change your responses. An autopilot response is quick and allows you to move on, even though it is not necessarily your best self.

If you want to grow beyond these autopilot responses for surviving, you need a strategy to override them. Simply put, many of these reflexes are not healthy when it comes to caring about yourself and building relationships. Remember, choosing a behavior or substance to cope helps you manage an unwanted feeling or situation. It helps you survive. But surviving does not look very pretty. When you cope, you are focused on comforting or protecting yourself. You can often hurt others by how you talk or what you do. You probably do not end up liking yourself so well, either. And most likely, your response does not represent the person God created you to be.

Thriving, on the other hand, depends on being intentional. The person you want to become is likely not the one who shows up when you are mad, sad, lonely, scared, or ashamed. When you are intentional, you slow down enough to make a conscious decision of how you want to respond to situations. You consciously practice responding in ways that represent the person you long to be. The more you behave and respond to life circumstances in ways that reflect the person you want to be, the more you like yourself. The more you thrive.

"I've realized I focus on the urgent, not the important!" said one of my clients. She was beginning to understand the difference between surviving and thriving. Hers was a reactionary lifestyle, not a proactive, intentional way of living. I lived this way most of the time before I entered my own journey of healing. I did not know there was a different way to live than to wait for things to happen and then respond to them. There were so many things to respond to as a busy mom of three little ones that I usually did not get to other important matters in my life. I slowly began to lose myself in that kind of living.

A proactive life is an intentional life. You make decisions about what you want to do and how you want to respond in situations. You create a vision for becoming the person you want to be. It is forward thinking. It is motivated from within, not from what others want for you. When you are proactive, you initiate what is important to you. "Those who live in accordance with the Spirit have their minds set on what the Spirit desires" (Rom. 8:5). An intentional life is moving through life and making decisions in sync with the Holy Spirit. You like who you are. You feel peace and contentment as you slowly become the person God calls you to be.

There is no better time to be challenged to be intentional than when you are facing adversity, when life is difficult. I have had clients say to me that, in their pain, they hated who they had become. That is understandable. Pain leads you to react quickly, and that behavior is often not representative of the person you know yourself to be. No matter what others do or say, how *do* you want to be? Do you like your response? If not, you can work on changing how you respond.

I have noticed that people who do not work on changing unhealthy responses become *more so* in those responses as they grow older. If you are impatient in frustrating situations and do not work on changing that, in your elder years you will probably display even more impatience. If you blame others regularly when you are mad, your blaming only will grow. If you withdraw to cope with hurt, you will no doubt withdraw more. If you see the world from a critical, negative perspective, you will probably see it more negatively as you age. As I have grown older and spend more time visiting family in senior communities, I see it! It is a stark reminder to keep working on these things. I want my *more so* to be gentleness and kindness and joy and patience. What do you want your *more so* to be?

Ask Yourself: What Disturbs My Peace?

Finding peace is one of the best ways to thrive. Living with love, joy, and peace is a good description of thriving, don't you think? So many Scriptures tell us that this is what God wants for us too. *Jesus Calling* by Sarah Young has many daily reminders of how you can ground yourself in God's truths.

> Peace is my continual gift to you. It flows abundantly from My throne of grace. Just as the Israelites could not store up manna for the future but had to gather it daily, so it is with My Peace. The day-by-day collecting of manna kept My people aware of their dependence on Me. Similarly, I give you sufficient Peace for the present when you come to me "by prayer and petition, with thanksgiving" (Phil. 4:6). If I gave you permanent Peace, independent of My Presence, you might fall into the trap of self-sufficiency. May that never be![1]

God wants us to live in peace. After all, he is the Prince of Peace. I look at every slice of my day to see if there is peace and joy. If my peace is disturbed, then I name what I am feeling and what I think I need. I also invite the Holy Spirit into my plan, either to bless it or change it. And then I go after *doing* what I can to find more peace. This is where I also need to remember to take responsibility for what I can change—myself, not another person. If your peace depends on someone else changing something about their life, you could ask for it or encourage it. If they do not comply, you will want to have a plan for something you can do for yourself.

I was very tired recently, and my to-do list was growing long. I'd planned to leave for a three-day trip to visit family, but when I listened to a quiet voice within whisper, *You could shorten your trip,* I knew it was the Holy Spirit leading me. As soon as I changed my plans, I immediately felt at peace. The extra time gave me a chance to slow down and rest, prioritize my to-do list, and eliminate some unnecessary tasks.

A friend told me her job was exhausting her. The negative energy from all the customer complaints she was handling left her lifeless at the end of each day. Listening to God's promptings, she told me, meant she had to quit, despite not having another plan for work. She rested, talked to others about her fear of not having enough money, made a plan for pursuing other work, and decided to trust God to help her with future plans. Her energy and presence to people she cared about returned. She felt great peace. And within six weeks, she was offered two promising jobs.

The classic Serenity Prayer gives us a great reminder about peace:

> God grant me the Serenity to accept the things I cannot change, the Courage to change the things I can, and the Wisdom to know the difference.[2]

When my peace is disturbed, I first name the things I cannot change or control. "I *cannot* stop someone from looking at pornography." "I *cannot* stop the spread of the COVID-19 virus." "I *cannot* know the reason my husband died at such a young age." "I *cannot* guarantee that people will always be there for me."

Then I explore the things I *can* change. "I *can* decide if I will stay with someone who continues to be unfaithful to me." "I *can* take precautions to keep myself as safe as possible from the COVID-19 virus." "I *can* trust that God has a plan for me after the death of my husband." "I *can* learn how to take care of myself and not be afraid if others cannot."

"Wisdom to know the difference" means that I do not fight against what is true. I accept it. I do what I can and am grateful to have choices. And then I ask God to help me with the things I cannot do or understand. There is peace that comes from knowing I have done all I know to do. I have not been passive. And when I am in an active place but still do not have the solution or peace I long for, I can take hold of the wisdom in knowing I am not out of options. I still have God, who has ideas and plans far beyond what I could ever dream of. I will trust that he is always with me and for me, leading me to my next right step.

Take the Next Right Step

Finding peace in your life gets easier if you practice living in the present. This concept has become particularly popular these days. *Mindfulness* is the word currently being used in the mental health field. It encourages you to focus on what is here, right now, rather than the past or the future. That can be a challenge when you have faced adversity or trauma. There will be times when you need to look back to work through the emotions of loss and to grieve. Looking at the future is also important when you need to consider your priorities, vision, and changes you want to work on. Often the pain you are experiencing in the present can paralyze you from knowing what to do next. A participant in one of our workshops called this "future tripping." If you get so consumed about what you are going to do or what might happen in a week, a month, or a year from now, you can rob yourself of paying attention to your next right step.

Sometimes we use language like "I had an intuition," or a "gut feeling," or a "red flag" to describe this internal place of knowing. As a Christian, I believe these experiences are the Holy Spirit grabbing our attention, trying to tell us something or direct us to do something. *Your* next right step might be different from someone else's next right step. It usually is. There is no one right way to respond to any given circumstance. When a newly betrayed woman asks me what she should do, for example, we talk about some possibilities, and then I teach her about the Spirit within her whom I want her to listen for. That, I say, is where you will connect to *your* next right step. I then tell her I will help her discern that while she is practicing. You can learn to listen for *your* direction. Discernment usually happens when you are quieted and can hear the still small voice of God.

In 1 Kings we read the story of the prophet Elijah fleeing from Jezebel when she threatened his life. Elijah had confronted King Ahab and his supporters about following Baal and not God. When Ahab told his wife, Queen Jezebel, about all Elijah had said, she was furious and planned to have him killed. Elijah fled to Mount Horeb, and eventually, it was there that he heard from God. The Lord told him to go out on the mountain because he was going to pass by. He wanted Elijah to hear what he had to say. Elijah experienced a powerful wind, an earthquake, and then a fire. But the Lord was not in any of those experiences. And then we are told a gentle whisper came, and the Lord was in the whisper (19:11–13).

How often do you expect that you will know your next right step only after some miraculous or powerful event happens in your life? Perhaps instead you might quiet your soul and humble your heart so you do not miss the gentle whisper of God. That has been when I most often hear my next right step.

One of the hardest challenges for many of us is the pace of life. It is fast and full. There are few margins. You are stretched out like a taut rubber band, ready to snap if there is one more thing to do. How could you begin to hear a holy whisper? So your next right step might be deciding how you will find stillness in your life (Ps. 46:10). Thankfully, one of the benefits of pain is that it slows us down. Consider that a gift instead of fighting it. Know that God has a plan for you when you are still. He needs to talk to you—regularly. Each right step will bring a small slice of peace. And then there will be another, and another. You will begin to feel calmer and, hopefully, trust in this wise counsel.

Your next right step will get clearer as you get closer to it, because it will lead you to peace. Eventually you will not need to say, "My counselor told me to do this," or "I read in this great book that this is what I should do," or "All my friends will think I'm crazy if I don't act soon." Others' opinions will not direct your paths; the still small voice will. Of course, that does not mean you do not seek help or advice from others. And you will know it is *your* next right step because it will be followed by peace.

I talked with a client yesterday who was facing her husband's relapse after several years. She thought she needed to separate from him to "teach him a lesson." I asked her if she needed space and time for herself to process the pain of her husband's relapse. She said she did not, really, because it was also true that they were talking deeply and sharing in good conversations. She did not want to miss out on that. However, she thought that if she did not create some greater consequence for him, he probably would not change. We talked about her motivation and the difference in taking the next right step for herself versus taking a step to change him. And we talked about which decision—to separate or to stay—brought her the most peace in that moment. Her answer came quickly: "To stay." She agreed that this was the direction of her spirit in this moment. *And* it might change in the future. She would stay connected to that possibility too.

Sometimes we miss the message, and our next step does not bring us peace! If that happens, God will be patiently waiting, just like our GPS system when we have missed a turn. The voice calmly tells us, "Make a U-turn at the next intersection." It will be no different in your life choices. You always have a choice to make another decision. Eventually peace will follow.

Consider Your Choices

You always have choices! As you grow, your choices will expand. We call that being *resourceful*. When a problem comes, a resourceful person will ponder many ways to solve it. You are not stuck with your life unless you want to be. You can learn to look for the choices you have. You can ask others to help you if you cannot see your alternatives. Slowing down and asking for God's help will provide even more choices.

Even when physical choices may be limited, you have a choice about your attitude and your beliefs. As Viktor Frankl writes, "Everything can be taken from a person but one thing: the last of the human freedoms—to choose one's attitude in any given set of circumstances, to choose one's own way."[3] I know God is there for me, providing for me all the desires of my heart—eventually. This allows me to be patient in the moment when things are not working out or my requests are seemingly not being answered. My trust in God has grown through many trying times. He will provide choices and relay them to me in his still small voice.

A life of surviving is often filled with bitterness, resentment, regret, and loss. As people build more walls of protection and coping behaviors, they can lose connection with others and their own passion and purpose. They may experience a hardened heart and a lack of trust in anyone, including God. It is a cautious, suspicious, joyless life.

You can have a life of thriving. Start by taking responsibility for your life and working on being authentic. Know what you feel and listen to the messages your emotions are telling you about what you need. Learn how to be clear and direct about your needs and desires, not always expecting your spouse or family to take care of all of them. Be willing to change the ways you cope with difficult emotions that do not contribute to your well-being or your relationships. Listen for God's quiet whisper to direct your next right steps so that you can stay present to this day, not all the future days that you cannot control. Find peace and joy even in adversity, especially as you experience God's hand at work in the details of your life. Peace, calm, patience, openness, and joy can be yours if you want to thrive. I believe this is the definition of healing from something hard or traumatic.

———————

This chapter has offered many options to help you thrive. You don't need to do all of them at once. Choose one that seems suited to your needs and focus there. Having community with others who desire to heal from adverse situations will make the process much more enjoyable. And you can practice with each other. Remember, this is not a sprint. This is a lifelong decision to practice working on becoming your best self. A traumatic experience may end up being the thing that directs your time and energy to a new venture.

> ▶ Turn to the Gentle Assignments section on page 173 for further reflection.

5

Exploring You—The Person You Take Everywhere

An unexamined life is not worth living.

Socrates

IF I HAD NOT EXPERIENCED THE PAIN of relational betrayal, I do not think I would have taken the time or used what little money we had as a young couple to start exploring my life. There were many happy aspects of my life—a loving husband, three beautiful children, and involvement in my neighborhood, church, and schools. Life was not perfect, *and* it was very good. I could have been paralyzed by thoughts that counseling was for people who had problems. I did not believe, when Mark's addictive life was uncovered, that *I* had things to work on. I believed *he* had things to work on. He was the one who needed counseling!

In my early therapy appointments, however, I experienced the empowerment of "knowing myself." I could change. Trauma could lead me to transforming the person I was, even if I had not caused the trauma. I found so much room to grow—to become the person God called me to be. Exploring my life was not about judging me. It was not about condemnation or confrontation. It was not about finding fault for others' problems within me. It was an invitation to live with more contentment, more joy, more authenticity, more passion, and more purpose. It was an invitation to grow closer to other people, to be known, to use the gifts and talents God had given me, to have peace within and love for life and others. I was stirred at my core when my journey led me here. Deep down I wanted more in my life, *and* I did not know how to articulate it or seek it. My pain created a path to lead me.

Life-changing counseling or study helps you look at *you*. It helps you figure out why you do what you do, think what you think, and feel what you feel. It helps you understand *you*. Examination can help you decide what you want to change and how to go about it. Counseling was not about making me responsible for Mark's addiction. Everyone makes choices to manage pain in certain ways. Others have 100 percent responsibility for what they choose to do, and we have 100 percent responsibility for our own choices.

You may be saying, "What I really want is for someone to figure out my spouse. When I tell my counselor all the crazy, hurtful things he does, I want my counselor to validate that *he* needs to change!" You may start out in that place. However, effective counsel will help you know yourself better. You learn to make healthier choices and, ideally, become a person who keeps growing and loving your life. Changing *you* is the only part of life you can control. And changing *you* does change your relationships too, because you are part of a system. A system is interconnected, like a mobile: when one dangling part is touched, all the other parts start moving. Your relationships—marriage, family, friendships—are like that as well. You affect one another. You cannot change one part without causing change in the others as well. If you scream at someone in your "system," they will probably move away from you. If someone in your system is a good listener, you will probably talk with them more. There are continual interactions in your relationships, and you can start any of them!

Your Identity

You might believe that your traumatic life experiences identify who you are, and you will carry a label or a defect forever. You may feel shame about what happened to you. You may believe you cannot change, and say, "I've always been this way. It's just who I am." When you examine your life, new possibilities appear and new beliefs are formed. You can create new character and new behaviors . . . a new identity.

I am a twin. Something as simple as our names—Barb coming earlier in the alphabet than Debbie—created numerous situations when Barb would go first. I was comforted by her experiencing events before I did. That became normal. Barb was also more outgoing than me, so she engaged in activities while I often watched. I seemed to be more innately cautious than Barb. I believe these experiences and many others contributed to my becoming a follower, while Barb became a leader. I continued this pattern for many years and eventually married a strong leader. I was comfortable in my role as a follower. Do you see how my experiences may have influenced that choice? It was not about abuse or neglect, just ordinary life events. Once I took time to explore this, I decided that I had leadership talents too. I made changes, which required getting out of my comfort zone. I became the CEO of a company I founded with a friend. I learned how to travel alone, take care of finances, make difficult decisions, and parent by myself when my husband was away. I learned how to write a book! And today, I am leading Faithful & True, the counseling center Mark and I cofounded. Today, I claim leading as part of who I want to be.

It is easy to let others determine your identity by what *they* believe. Did your parents want you to be in sports when your heart was in art? Were you required to study piano when you loved playing the drums? Were you pressured into a career that was someone else's choice for you but not really yours? Maybe you were influenced to stay at home with your family when you thrived at working outside the home. I hear these stories regularly in my practice. People are not happy with their lives. Perhaps they have not had enough encouragement to follow their passion and purpose and are following someone else's. Or perhaps, in the busyness of attending to responsibilities, they have not had the time to know what they like or are passionate about. If this describes you, you know that discontentment at a heart level can lead to coping, anxiety, and depression. *And* it can be a reminder that you have choices and want to change something!

Your Safety and Worth

Your sense of safety and worth began developing the day you were born. Psychologists and therapists call this your *attachment style*. It is a set of basic assumptions, or core beliefs, about yourself and others. There has been extensive research looking at infants and toddlers and how their mothers interact with them. These early life experiences determine if a child knows they are worthy of being loved—or not—and that others are reliable and trustworthy—or not. How you were attended to—or not—has led to your sense of safety and worth.[1]

If you lived with abusive or neglectful parents, siblings, or other significant people in your life, you likely believed people were not trustworthy, they were unavailable to help you, and you were not worthy. In an unexamined life, you carry those beliefs with you as you move through life. You might marry someone who repeats those patterns of abuse or neglect, or someone who is exactly the opposite, unconsciously believing they will be safer. If you grew up in a home where there was considerable yelling and confrontation, you may choose a spouse who sounds exactly like that—repeating the pattern from your family. It may also be that you marry someone who is extremely quiet and rarely shares feelings, thoughts, or needs. That would be the opposite of your experiences, and seemingly much safer. The truth is, neither provide the secure attachment and safety you desire. The good news is you can change that in your adult relationships. It is possible. *And* it takes help and time.

Your Voice

It is easy to lose your voice about things that matter to you . . . and to eventually lose yourself in the process. There are many life experiences that contribute to your being quiet, or "losing your voice," as counselors often say. When this happens, you may notice you are not being authentic about what you are feeling, thinking, or needing at times. That is how you lose yourself. Slowly, slowly, part of you dies every time you silence yourself. Sometimes you may have been told to be "seen and not heard" in your own family. Or your faith journey suggests you should only care about others' needs and not focus on your own. Sometimes you do not believe you are important enough to speak up about yourself. It is no doubt a pattern that started early in life and became so normal you never think about it—until one day you do. That is the beginning of self-exploration that can lead to a healthier you.

Your Story

When you tell your story, you put together a narrative of your life events. It is an account of your life. Sharing your story allows others to know you. Your story will include not just the experiences you had (good and bad) but also what you *believed* about each experience and what you *did* about it. If you follow these beliefs and responses into your adulthood, you'll notice you are carrying some of the same beliefs and the same responses—until such time as you examine them and decide to change them.

When I was four, my twin sister and I were in a ballet performance in front of many family members. Barb was facing the wrong direction, and in hopes of helping her out, I tiptoed down the line and turned her around. I thought it was a very loving thing to do. The audience broke out in snickers of laughter, and it became a story shared many times over at family gatherings. It did not seem funny to me. I felt embarrassed and ashamed, believing I had done something wrong and was stupid. I responded by not saying anything and just withdrew. I never wanted to talk about it, and I did not. Do you see how an innocent, small event can lead to a strong "core belief" about yourself or others? I carried a fear that if I did something "stupid," people would laugh at me and think I was dumb. I was overcautious and risk-adverse for many years. Perhaps this event contributed to my behavior. Counseling directed me to a new belief and a new response that is true and freeing. I can still feel that fear when I am in public settings! Today I can choose to believe something different, *and* it is hard.

Only by intentionally watching yourself will you know that you can intentionally change yourself. You are not your experiences, especially the traumatic ones. You can change how you respond to events. You can change what you believe.

God wants what is best for you. After all, you were "fearfully and wonderfully made" (Ps. 139:14), created in God's image, filled with passion and purpose, uniquely designed with special gifts and talents—a lovable, chosen treasure. God so loved you that he sent his Son to die for you, knowing you would not live perfectly. God already thought about that. You are covered. You are just encouraged to keep using trials and adversity to become the person he called you to be. He wants you to be intentional about transforming trials. He wants you to live loved. He wants you to find peace in all situations.

As your story continues to unfold, the hope is you will use all experiences to learn about yourself and decide what needs changing. If you want to be the best version of yourself, there will undoubtedly be things you will want to change. No one leads a perfect life. And no one can say they have nothing to change. And if they do . . . pride might be the issue! Do you have a desire to grow and be a better person—as a spouse, mother, sister, daughter, friend, colleague, daughter of God? A journey of self-examination can lead you there.

▶ Turn to the Gentle Assignments section on page 174 for further reflection.

6

Practical Steps to Exploring You

> When we are no longer able to change a situation, we are challenged to change ourselves.
>
> Viktor E. Frankl

HERE ARE SOME PRACTICAL STEPS to examine your life. Each one will give you an opportunity to know yourself better. You can decide if you want to change something to become more authentic and connected to the *you* God intended you to be. This is not an exhaustive list. Beware of becoming overwhelmed by the topics. You can read through them quickly if you like, then return and focus on one at a time. You might find a friend who wants to explore the list with you and have discussions about each section. A counselor could help you as well. Please be gentle with yourself as we dive in together.

Be a Gentle Observer

Maureen Graves, who was a gifted counselor for me when I was traumatized by infidelity, used a great phrase: be a "gentle observer."

You can start by being a gentle observer of yourself. Watch yourself as if you are sitting in a corner taking notes about who you are, how you respond to things, what you say to others, and what you say to yourself. There is no judgment about this information, just noticing. Cali, my fourteen-year-old rescued kitty, reminds me of an accomplished gentle observer. She sits on her little cube in the corner of the kitchen and watches people come and go. She knows whom to meow to for different things because she has observed what works with whom—food, treats, brushing, lap sitting. She knows to run under the chair when the vacuum starts. She knows nap locations where no one will bother her. She knows who needs comfort because she feels their sadness. That is the essence of a gentle observer.

Observing can enlighten you about many aspects of yourself. You might see yourself being quiet when people around you are getting very loud. You might get critical when someone does not follow through with something you asked of them. You might think you are regularly doing more than your share of work. Maybe you notice that you have little patience with people who do not seem to try hard. You might get resentful when people are not appreciative of things you do for them. Perhaps you do not show sadness very often, but you are easily angered. You may observe that you are not happy most days and do not really like yourself very much. You may become aware that you do not know what you like very often; you default to what others like. Being a gentle observer is the beginning of self-exploration. It will give you information to decide what to do next.

Try to have some "fun" observing yourself. Get to know who you are. After all, you are the person you take everywhere! You take yourself to gatherings with friends. You decide what opportunities you will expose yourself to. You enter marriage with your experiences, beliefs, and expectations. You let yourself have fun—or not—depending upon your beliefs about work and play. You believe in yourself—or not. You love yourself—or not. Most importantly, you have the power to help yourself change to become the best version of yourself. Observing yourself will allow you to name the things you want to change. Why? As Joanna Gaines entitled her children's book, *The World Needs Who You Were Made to Be.*

I had fun being a gentle observer in my life and saying, "Note to self: This is what I am noticing about you!" And then I put words to my notes: you often hold back what you are thinking instead of sharing; you have a tender heart; you are a mix of an introvert and an extrovert; you have many interests; you have a lot of energy; you have a lot of great ideas; you can give too much advice sometimes; you love to learn. These notes were things I wanted to revisit about who I was and what I wanted to work on changing—or not. Will you enjoy being a gentle observer of you? Remember, *gentle* does not mean critical or mean or judgmental. Being a gentle observer will help you care for the *you* who goes everywhere with you.

Consider Your Worth

Well-being and thriving start here. God created you in his image: "You are my Beloved, on you my favor rests."[1] He brought you into this world because he loves *you*. You are a delight to him. You are a treasure. He values you. You are worthy. You are his beloved. If you could bask in the beauty of who God created you to be, you could stop needing others to stoke your self-esteem. Unfortunately, that is a difficult task to ask of anyone, especially when others hurt us, exclude us, criticize us, blame us, or abuse us. Because we are human beings who sin and fall short, we do all these things to each other, even when we do not mean to. And we stop believing we are lovable or worthy. I can only imagine how sad God must be when this happens to his precious children.

I am reminded of how I feel as a parent of three wonderful children. Mark and I cherished these little ones from their inception.

We could not wait for them to enjoy life and claim their beloved-ness. And yet, I know they experienced the pain of rejection, of not being enough, of doubts about their worth. It saddens me greatly to think of them struggling with these thoughts. I know we did not parent perfectly. I know others hurt them too. I would like to think I can relate to God's sadness when you or I can-not accept the truth about who we are. As their parent, I want only for my children to know they are fearfully and wonderfully made. The world is waiting for them to be who God created them to be.

How are you doing with accepting that truth about yourself? I occasionally ask this question of women in my counseling groups. Do you know what I find? One hundred percent of them still struggle with believing in their belovedness—their value and worth—today. I know that discovery of infidelity can rock your foundation of self-esteem and worth. It is easy to say that because of the betrayal of your spouse, you no longer feel lovely, accept-able, or enough. Some say that they used to believe in the beauty of who they are, but this trauma has robbed them of that truth. I understand that. It was true for me too. And yet, I learned in my years of self-examination that if I really had been living in God's truth of me, *nothing* would have rocked me from that place. I had some work to do to figure out my story, the whole story from when I was little to the present, to understand all the ways I'd fallen away from God's truth about me. It was not just one adversity that did it.

I believe many people would love for others to build their self-esteem or worth by pouring lovely comments and affirmations over them: "If you would just tell me I am beautiful or accomplished or enough, maybe I would believe it." The problem is, creating self-esteem is an inside job. There are never enough compliments to change someone's belief about their worth if they do not believe it themselves. I am sure you have experienced this. You try to build someone up by telling them what a lovely person they are or how much you appreciate their gifts and talents, and it is like water rolling off a duck's back. It does not penetrate. This is a spiritual journey you must take until you are willing to accept God's truth about who you are. My hope is that as you work on yourself and love the more authentic, gentle person you are becoming, it will become easier to take in God's love for you, his treasure and beloved daughter.

I like to say it another way. Your self-esteem and worthiness are like a freshly baked cake. You are responsible for baking that cake. No one else can do that for you. It is true that, for some, past experiences have made it a lot harder to get started. Criticism, abuse, and abandonment have robbed you of some of the ingredients—the true beliefs about yourself. God has all the missing ingredients for you. When you reclaim them and get baking, you will have a beautiful, moist cake ready for decoration. Then you can let others decorate it with you, and those decorations will stick and will enhance the beauty of that beautiful cake.

One of the ways you notice your belovedness—or lack of it—is to examine how you talk to yourself. We all do it. Internally, we are constantly saying things to ourselves that no one else can hear. *I can't believe you did that. How stupid that you didn't catch that mistake. You're not smart enough to go back to school. You'll never be as pretty as those other women he spent time with. You aren't very interesting. You are not very lovable.* Self-talk is one of the ways you put yourself down. Henri Nouwen, a well-known spiritual writer, said in his book *Life of the Beloved*, "Over the years, I have come to realize that the greatest trap in our life is not success, popularity, or power, but self-rejection."[2] May you begin to love yourself as God loves you by being kind to yourself.

When you do not fully believe in your belovedness, you will seek others' approval. If someone else thinks you are pretty, then maybe you are. If someone else thinks you are smart, then maybe that is true. If someone else thinks you are enough, then maybe they will be kind, loving, or faithful to you. God continues to encourage you to seek his approval first and foremost. Are you doing that? Are you giving too much power to other earthlings? Are you checking in with the One who longs for you to live loved and to stop striving to please others? One of the biggest challenges to well-being will be trusting in your belovedness. "How can you love someone else if you do not love yourself?" as a song asks. You cannot love others well if you do not first love yourself as your Maker loves you. You will forever be covering up your shame—*I am not worthy*—with perfectionism, narcissism, or defensiveness that are not attractive to others. Take time to explore what happened in your life to rock you off this place of truth—*I am worthy and I am lovable.* I would venture to say it is not one person or one event but most likely a piling up of many life experiences.

Have the Courage to Be Imperfect

A colleague of Alfred Adler, one of the first psychologists practicing in the early 1900s, said, "Have the courage to be imperfect."[3] So many people struggle with perfectionism. When you are afraid to talk about what was imperfect, botched up, embarrassing, or a failure, you miss the opportunity to be human. You miss the chance to belong to your fellow human beings who are the same. Imperfect. If you were perfect, you would be God. And you are not. God encourages you to take the plank out of your own eye, no one else's eye (Matt. 7:3), and continue to work on becoming more Christlike. Period.

This is a simple reminder that if you are authentic, you will *own* the parts of your life that are not perfect. This means you will admit when you fall short, when you hurt someone, when you do not like how you behaved, and when you do not like who you are in the moment. Owning something suggests you will be willing to work on changing it. This is the best way to grow closer to other people. In case you missed it, people like the fact that you are normal, not supernatural! You make mistakes. You do not always treat people well. You have things to work on to be a better person. So, admit it. Have the courage to be imperfect.

Your own body and soul will like it too. It is exhausting to think you can live perfectly, create perfectly, or perform perfectly. What's the point? Your belief might be that if you could rise to such a level of living, you might finally be loved and accepted. That you would be worthy. You already are all those things. You sacrifice time and energy that might go to more worthy ventures, such as trying something new, spending more time with friends or family, doing self-care, and having fun. Give yourself a break. Work on those things that will make you a better person and know that you will never be perfect. As the saying goes, "Angels can fly because they can take themselves lightly."[4] You may need to lighten up so that you are more enjoyable to be with—and life is more enjoyable for you.

I love this saying so much that I had a friend create a piece of art for my office wall: "Have the courage to be imperfect." It is beautifully simple. And then I asked her to make another piece that says, "It is good enough!" When she'd given them to me, I was eager to hang them up. No measuring needed in my method of picture hanging. I grabbed my hammer and nails and went to work. The first piece hung perfectly. But when I eyeballed the nail for "It is good enough" and hung that piece, I could see it was off-center. I pulled the nail and tried again. The second nail had it tipping to the left. The next sent it tipping to the right. The nail holes continued until I thought I had it perfect—nine in all, hiding behind the picture frame! Then I sat down and had a good laugh at myself. Perfectionism is a tough one to overcome. I evidently am still working on it!

> Search me, God, and know my heart;
> test me and know my anxious thoughts.
> See if there is any offensive way in me,
> and lead me in the way everlasting. (Ps. 139:23–24)

Examine Your Cabinet of Core Beliefs

Core beliefs is a term used in the clinical world to describe what you are thinking about yourself, others, and the world. Your core belief system is connected to your feelings and your behaviors. It is like the engine of your car, central to the whole thing running smoothly and predictably. If you have not paid much attention to the engine of your car, you could be surprised by what it does one day: the sluggish starts you experienced finally led to a depleted battery; the engine light that warned you it was time for an oil change led to total engine failure. Sometimes you may not know what those "auto beliefs" are until you start exploring them. When I first started driving, I did not know that a squeak in my brakes meant they would soon need to be replaced. Only recently did I learn that sluggish starts could mean my battery was depleted. In the same way, we often do not pay attention to our core beliefs until we have a significant reaction to something.

Why can one person have little response to an event, and another has outright rage? Why do you get resentful about something, but someone else laughs about it? If you stop to ask people what they believe about any given life event, you will notice that their different feelings and responses connect to different beliefs. Here are some examples. When I am driving on several inches of fresh snow, my belief is that the roads are slippery and it will be easy to get into an accident. The feelings I have are fear and anxiety. My behavior that follows is to drive very slowly and to brake often to test out how slippery it is. Someone else may be a seasoned driver in a big truck with all-wheel drive and winter tires. When they are driving the same roads as me, their belief might be that the snow is not a problem and their vehicle is very safe. The feelings that accompany that belief are confidence and calm, so the behavioral outcome is to drive just as fast as usual. Two different beliefs have created two different emotional responses and two different behaviors. Beliefs, feelings, and behaviors are always connected. If you want to become a gentle observer of people's behaviors, start asking them about what they believe. I invite you to do the same for yourself.

Your core beliefs direct what you do. If you believe you are not smart, you may abandon pursuing a new career that interests you. If you believe you must do things perfectly, you may give up and not try new things, or you will work twice as hard as another person. If you believe you are not interesting, you may not engage in new relationships that could be fulfilling. If you believe a family member does not like you, you may stop communicating with them. If you believe you are not safe, you may create many boundaries that will keep people away from you. If you believe people must do things in a certain way, you will struggle with being with people who are different from you. Beliefs are not good or bad, right or wrong. They just are. They will lead you to decide what you will do. You may not be aware that is happening, *and* it is. Your beliefs drive your decisions about how you will live.

What is also true is that beliefs of others are being poured into you from the moment of your birth. That can be good in that we all need help learning about life and how to manage it. "Eat good food, not just junk food." "Share your toys." "Don't run into the street without looking." "Be kind to others." "Trust that I will come back." "God loves you." All of these are beliefs.

And they keep coming, from parents, siblings, friends, teachers, and pastors. "Dress like that and boys will take advantage of you." "Listen to that music and you will contaminate your life." "Live perfectly so that God will love you." "Be sexual before marriage because everybody is." "Don't be sexual before marriage because God wants you to be pure." You accumulate a whole "cabinet of beliefs," as I like to say. They are all stacked up in there, informing you of how to live your life. We do not often stop to examine them, and so they drive us to behave or make choices automatically.

85

Here are some examples of beliefs that drove my life:

If you are a good person, you will be responsible with money.

Do not trust people too much. (I grew up in the Chicago suburbs.)

Tell people where you are going when you leave.

Don't boast about yourself or you will look egotistic.

Work first. Play later.

If things get too hard, wait, and time will heal things.

Always look your best.

Don't be angry. Don't be in conflict.

Men are very sexual—don't lead them on.

Outside work is for men. Inside work is for women.

Be cautious. Life is dangerous.

There are hundreds of these beliefs in my cabinet. Have you ever gone into your pantry or kitchen shelves and started looking at expiration dates? It can be astonishing. Something led me to do that recently, and I found cans and boxes of food that were ten years old . . . or more! Beliefs about yourself, others, and the world can be like that. Outdated. You may be carrying around beliefs you simply do not want to live with today. They do not represent the person you want to be or the life you want to live. Your job as an adult today is to figure out what might be outdated. Receiving counseling or talking to others who also want to explore their beliefs can help. Sometimes we do not think to believe something else because our belief has been with us for a long time. It is familiar. Our environment and belief systems become normal. Hearing stories of what others believe can be the impetus to exploring other possibilities.

What do you believe about money, gender roles, success, God/religion, trust, having needs, accepting help, privacy, anger, lying, authority, fun, and feelings? You could start by making a list of these things and seeing what your current beliefs are about them. There are plenty of other categories too. As I mentioned before, have some fun getting to know yourself and what you believe. It can make for interesting conversations with others as well. I've had some of the best talks with my mom, who recently turned 101, when I've asked her what beliefs she grew up with.

You might notice that the beliefs you did not like growing up are opposite for your spouse or the people you befriend. We often find relationships to help us change or fine-tune our beliefs so we can clean out the outdated ones. If you grew up with many limitations on what you could do, you might connect with others who love adventure and exploration. If you were taught to save money whenever possible, you might enjoy a relationship with someone who spends money more freely. If you were told family members should live close to each other, you may marry someone whose job takes you far away. It is also possible that you choose people to be around whose beliefs are like yours. There is always a combination of cleaning out what is outdated and keeping what is good. There are so many beliefs in your cabinet. Explore your cabinet and the relationships that are helping you clean out or preserve your beliefs.

I have a flower bucket in my office that says, "Be a possibilitarian." I love that word. It reminds me to consider other possible beliefs about what I see. I can get stuck in believing that my thinking—or belief—is the truth. And everybody ought to believe the same way. My journey over the years has led me to be a possibilitarian and ask, "Why else might that person be doing or saying that?" There are numerous stories or possibilities that could be true if we slow down and ponder them. The best solution is to ask that person. When a good friend of mine had not texted or called for a long time, I was tempted to think, *I bet I did something to annoy her.* I decided to check out that possibility. When I asked her if I had done something to annoy her because

I had not heard back from her in a long time, she said, "Oh dear, no! My granddaughter just had surgery, and I got distracted with helping the family. I am so sorry I have not communicated. I really miss you." It was good to know there was another possibility. If an adolescent is misbehaving, you might believe they are a bad person. But it is also possible they are longing for attention because they are sad or mad about something. Any attention might be better than no attention. If your husband is looking at pornography, you might believe you are not attractive enough for him. It is also possible that he is searching for relief from old woundedness, and it is not about you at all.

You can be a possibilitarian too. Begin to imagine other possibilities when you see behaviors that are unsettling to you. Check out what you are believing. Listen for what is true. Possibilities are thoughts that are developing. They are beliefs stirring within that may or may not be true. A possibilitarian is a gentler, less judgmental, and more empathetic person—all qualities of thriving.

Find Yourself

You might not even realize you lost yourself along the way. If you are not aware, this "lostness" may show up as depression, overwhelmedness (I just made up that word), listlessness, over-involvement in others' lives, or lack of passion or purpose in who you were created to be. You may notice that you are happy only when those around you are happy. That you have things to do when others have need of you. You may not even know what you really like, what you would do, or what gives you meaning if you were to stand back and examine your life as a stand-alone person. Sometimes you only know who you are when you are attached to other people and doing what they need you to do. A client of mine once said, "I'm a giver: I gave away all of myself . . . and was lost."

I have a little Hello Kitty figure on my office shelf. Do you remember when they were so popular? This kitty has a cute little face, *and* she is missing her mouth. She reminds me that not speaking can lead to not being. You may have "lost your voice" about things that matter to you. In other words, you do not always speak up when you are sad, lonely, angry, confused, or scared. You may have experienced that it is not safe to talk about certain topics as people respond angrily or dismiss you. You may believe it does not matter if you talk about what you want or need because there are not ears to hear. You may just do what you do because it is easier, or it keeps the peace. You may not have the energy to focus on yourself because you are exhausted by all the responsibility you have for your children or spouse or work. Whatever may have happened to you in your story of living, there is part of you that begs to be reclaimed—or perhaps claimed for the first time. That is the part of you that is joyful, interesting, and energized. It is engaged in your gifts and talents, your creative side, your passion and purpose. It compels people to want to be around you and share life with you. It is life-giving, not life-draining. It is authentic. It is not hiding feelings, thoughts, or needs. It allows others to know you. You are simply being yourself and liking who that is. When you like who you are, many others will most likely like you too.

Your well-being depends upon you claiming and loving yourself. When I entered counseling over thirty years ago, my counselor, Maureen, had me find two pictures of myself when I was young. I was to carry one in my wallet so I would look at the picture when I was out and about. And she directed me to frame the other (ideally in a beautiful, sparkly frame) and place it somewhere I would pass by regularly. Maureen said, "Let her remind you that she wants to be loved and nurtured and to lead a joyful life. Be there for her. Be the wise woman who pours into her all that she desires. Even if she faced trials and trauma in her early life, you can be there for her now to make her future different. The past does not have to determine her future."

Consider Your Brain Health

There has been an explosion of information and focus on neurochemistry in the past few decades. Conferences, professional research and articles, books, and brain imaging all remind us that how our brain is functioning will significantly determine how we are functioning. As Daniel Amen, psychiatrist and author of many books on brain health, has said, "When your brain works well, you work well."[5]

Psychiatrists have been treating the brain for many years by analyzing patients' verbal reports of symptoms. They have not looked at the brain to decide how to treat mental health concerns. As Dr. Amen professes, "How can we know how to treat the brain if we do not look at it?" No other organ in the body is treated this way. We always look—through X-rays, MRIs, or CT scans. As he has said, similar mental health symptoms like anxiety, depression, mood disorders, or ADHD can be caused by different brain systems either overfunctioning or underfunctioning, and we will not know unless we look. This is what has led to Dr. Amen's career of thirty-plus years in brain imaging.[6]

All this to say, many experiences affect what your brain looks like and how it is functioning. At birth, some of the genetics from your family were passed on to you. ADHD, for instance, carries a genetic component. If a child is diagnosed with it, at least one parent has also lived with that brain health issue. Anxiety often runs through generations of families, as do tendencies for depression or obsessive-compulsive disorder (OCD). Additionally, early life trauma can impact the brain, and exposure to toxins in the environment, nutrition, level of physical activity, use of drugs and alcohol, and sleep all affect brain health.

Sometimes, if you are frustrated with a part of you that you do not like, the health of your brain may be a contributor. The great news is that your brain is malleable. It can change. This was not the belief many years ago, but today, psychiatrists and researchers know this is true. What you put into your body and mind can create a better life for you.

Over fifteen years ago, Mark and I were introduced to Dr. Amen and his work in brain imaging. He invited both of us to have our brains scanned, and we agreed. It was a simple, pain-free experience. What was most remarkable was what he was able to tell each of us about our brains despite having relatively little personal relationship with us at that time. He could see that living with two children and a spouse with ADD symptoms stressed my limbic system. And furthermore, he could tell my brain "liked to be busy." That was me to a T! Before I entered a counseling program, I struggled with being a martyr, and I carried a lot of resentment because I believed I did more than my share of work most days. I squeezed a chore into every minute. I did not waste time. I had lists of my lists! I had plans, plans, and more plans to keep it all flowing nicely.

I've learned several things since then. First, I did not know how to state my needs and ask for help. Second, I liked to be busy because I felt better when I was. When I found ways to be busy, that fed my neurochemistry. It is true even today that I am happier when I am doing things, lots of things. I do not find joy in sitting around or watching television. Third, I am prone to be busy because my brain is very detail-oriented. I like organization and follow-through. I am extremely responsible. Those brain qualities can be good at times, and at other times they do not make me a fun person. I work at slowing down because it does not come naturally to me. That is funny even as I write it! And it is true.

What kind of brain do you have? Do you know if you struggle with anxiety, depression, OCD, PTSD, sleep disorders, or other mental health issues? Do you know that getting help can change your brain and can lead to a healthier life? Sometimes you can get stuck by self-sabotaging thoughts like, *That's just the way I am*, or *It's not that bad*, or *Many members of my family are anxious*. When you are motivated to do all that you can to heal from trials and trauma in your life, I want to encourage you to look at this component too. You do not need to live with the brain you have. There are many books written about neurochemistry and brain health. You can also watch YouTube videos or listen to podcasts. Educate yourself by exploring this important organ of your body. Having a healthy brain is essential to your well-being.

Off-Load Your Emotions

Counselors describe a person's ability to regulate their emotions as "emotional regulation." What this means is that when you do experience feelings, you have tools or healthy behaviors to express them without repressing them completely or letting them appear out of control. You are regulated. Not knowing what you feel or not being able to share what you feel is not the same as regulating your emotions. However, if emotions get too big, they can be scary or not taken seriously and can drive people away (I think of Kramer from *Seinfeld*). You may only be able to express certain emotions regularly, like the positive ones of excitement, gratitude, and joy (I think of the eponymous Pollyanna). Or maybe you primarily express the negative ones, like sadness, hopelessness, and caution (I think of Eeyore from *Winnie the Pooh*). When you are consistently calm, there is no obvious expression of feelings (I think of someone being called a "Steady Eddie"). In any of these situations, counselors would use the term *emotional dysregulation*. Ideally, you can feel and talk about all your emotions in a safe way so that you are heard and understood. Working on your own well-being includes working on your emotional regulation.

As you get better at knowing what you feel, it will be helpful to find ways to off-load your emotions in a healthy way. Emotions take up residence inside of you, stirring around and deciding whether they will come out and spew over others or whether they will stay inside and mess with your health. They do not just go away. They can be dormant for a long time, though the truth is they are always there in some way, perhaps causing you to be irritable, moody, short-tempered, or shut down, or having some other presence that is hard to live with. Or maybe you are managing physical symptoms related to pent-up feelings inside your body. I am not saying that all physical ailments are caused by feelings, *and* I also know many people feel physically better after they have focused over time on releasing feelings more consistently and in a healthier way. I was surely one of those people.

Two emotions we all have that can drive our behaviors in unhealthy directions are anxiety and anger. Let's take a few minutes to explore them. Please remember that these emotions are difficult ones for everyone to manage. There is always room to grow in Christlike character when working on anger and anxiety. There is no shame or judgment with where you are—just encouragement to look at these two feelings and decide if there is anything you want to change.

Where Do You Rev?

If we are living and breathing, we will have some anxiety. And it is good that we do, because it warns us that something is potentially dangerous. It helps protect us and keeps us safe. When we are not feeling safe, some level of anxiety or fear will appear. Safety involves having the basics to live—food, shelter, money—and take care of yourself. Health issues and mortality are safety concerns, and one of the greatest fears for anyone is the fear of being all alone. If you regularly feel anxious, there is not something wrong with you; it simply means you perceive things in your world to be unsafe. What you may not be aware of is how often that feeling shows up for you, and when it does, what you do in response.

For most people, an attempt to control something when you do not feel safe is a very natural reaction. Have you ever been called a controlling person? Most likely, you are someone who has a significant amount of anxiety about something. The COVID-19 pandemic brought out anxiety in many people. *Should I leave my house? Will I die if I get the virus? Will I lose my job? How will I pay for my bills? Do I have enough supplies if stores close? Will the world ever seem normal again?* These are all issues of safety. If you were sexually abused by a significant male in your life, your safety was challenged too. *Will I ever be able to trust men again? Will I be able to be around him at family events and take care of myself? Will I be rejected if I talk about this with others? Will I always feel this much pain?* These issues of safety create anxiety. Being a gentle observer of yourself will inform you of what you do when you are anxious or do not feel safe. Eventually you can decide if you like what you are doing to manage your anxiety or if you would like to work on changing your reaction.

Anxiety can be debilitating and can interfere with relationships. How you handle your anxiety will affect your well-being. I ask my clients, "On a scale of 1–10, where do you rev with anxiety?" When a car engine revs, it races, just like your heart may race when you are anxious. If you are typically revving at a 7 or 8, it might mean you are anxious about many things throughout the day, and it effects your decisions regularly. If your spouse says he revs at about a 2 or 3, it probably means he does not worry much or carry much anxiety as he moves throughout his day. His focus is on what he wants or needs to do—much more carefree and content, perhaps. Anxiety in a relationship has a way of trumping much of what else is going on. In other words, an anxious person creates an environment that often requires other people to tend to their needs or emotions. Or they have resistance to doing things or going places because of their anxiety. It can be frustrating for the person who has lower anxiety, partly because they do not understand the needs of a highly anxious person, and because the person with more anxiety usually drives the decisions of the couple.

My dad was a pilot in WWII and loved flying his small L4 spotter plane (which was extremely dangerous!). My mom was afraid of little planes and refused to fly with him unless it was a commercial flight. I've always felt sad that they might have enjoyed some adventures renting a plane and flying somewhere. My mom's anxiety drove that decision. My anxiety revs up when watching anything violent on television or in a movie. I tried a few times to go with Mark to a war movie or some scary adventure movie, and each time, I had to leave and wait outside! My anxiety drove our movie and TV choices.

Elevated anxiety can be caused by many things. Traumatic life events can escalate one's anxiety and sense of unsafety. Posttraumatic stress and its many symptoms cause ongoing anxiety. Another possible source is your inherited DNA from family members who struggle with anxiety. If you look back at your family tree, it can be surprising to see the patterns of anxiety that have come down through the generations. Anxiety shows up whenever your circumstances seem unsafe. It could be that you are walking alone and hear sounds behind you. Or you might feel pressured to participate in something when you aren't good at it. You might be in a new social situation and do not know anyone. Or perhaps you are late for a meeting and everyone else is already there. There are many everyday circumstances that may rev up your anxiety, even though they might not for another person. What is most important to remember is that through more exploration, you can *do* something to change your level of anxiety if you desire.

The most important step to changing something is first acknowledging it. Then you can decide to do something. Taking an online assessment could help you see if anxiety is a problem for you. Also reading about anxiety can educate you about its symptoms. Your doctor can talk with you about possible medications. Counseling helps many people identify the roots of their anxiety. Integrative therapies are available to help you reduce stress and anxiety too. You do not need to live with an emotion that robs you of your well-being. Will you remember that you are not alone if this is an issue for you? Many people would love to live with less anxiety. It is common.

How Do You Respond When Angry?

There are many ways anger presents itself. Sometimes it is an aggressive physical expression: you hit things or people, throw things, slam doors, restrain people, or force others to do things they do not want to do. We are witnessing more and more physical expressions of anger in our culture, with people getting hurt or killed. It all feels frightening and out of control. We call these forms of anger physical abuse or physical violence. They damage your sense of safety, and they damage relationships.

Anger can also express itself emotionally: you scream, belittle, blame, criticize, or shame others. Anger can also come out passively, which means it is not a direct expression of the feeling. Sarcasm is a form of passive anger. It is an angry statement covered up with humor, so it does not look so angry. *Sarcasm* literally means "to tear the flesh." As its recipient, it feels like a dagger to your heart, but if you acknowledge that the humor hurt you, the deliverer responds with, "Can't you take a joke?" There is no winning with sarcasm. Withdrawing is another form of passive anger. It is a choice to not talk at all. It is probably noticeable that something is wrong, and yet with no information, others are left to try to figure you out. *Stonewalling* is a term used to describe extensive withdrawal. It is ignoring another person and not talking—for days, perhaps. Although it is quiet, it is still deadly to a relationship. It is passive anger and is no more admirable than shouting or hitting. This kind of anger is emotionally abusive in relationships, and it also damages a sense of safety. In the same way that physically acting out anger prevents you from being your best self, so do emotionally abusive or passive forms of anger.

Anger is an emotion, and it is a messenger to you that you need something. It seems so simple, *and* it is true. If you want to reduce the anger you feel, you will want to explore what it is telling you—What do you need? When you begin to do something about your need and choose to do it with integrity, your anger dissipates over time, and you feel more alive and whole too.

Mary Ann felt angry every time she stepped into her car because her husband had admitted he had taken his affair partner in it several times when they met. As hard as Mary Ann tried to push it out of her mind and tell herself there was nothing she could do now, it was a constant trigger that would not leave her. I asked her, in a perfect world, what she needed. She immediately said, "I want to get rid of that car! But I know we cannot afford it." I asked her if she would be willing to tell her husband about her hurt and anger and discuss how they might get a different car. We talked about how to do that with integrity, so she would like how she presented herself and he could hear her without being scared away by her emotions.

The next week she came to our session almost giddy and checked in as feeling "very good." She told me that when she shared her need with her husband, he willingly wanted to buy her a new car. He said they could make it work. And he encouraged her to pick out everything she wanted. He wanted to help her overcome this difficult trigger, and he was remorseful for causing her so much pain. Mary Ann ended by saying that she did not understand it, but she felt empowered by the whole situation. I believe empowered is what you feel when you can name a need and do something to get it met with integrity. I also believe that your emotions, including anger, are a nudge from the Holy Spirit that God wants something for you too. He wants you to claim legitimate needs and live with peace as much as possible.

Evie was pressured by her church community to come back to services, even though many had not yet received a COVID vaccine nor was the congregation taking precautions such as wearing masks and social distancing. She did not feel safe. She was frustrated and angry. In a perfect world, she would have loved for her pastor to take the guidelines for the pandemic more seriously and make changes at the church. Even though she spoke to him, she realized her need was not going to be met. She did not abandon her need, however. She and her husband decided they would drive to the church parking lot, sit in their car, and listen to the service on their tablet. In this way, they felt closer to their church community and could even wave when people walked by while still getting their need to feel safe met. I thought it was an ingenious solution. And Evie did not feel angry anymore because she had acted on her need.

You may need to grieve losses. Loss occurs whenever you have experienced change. The stages of grief include being angry. First comes shock and numbness, followed by a stage called *disorientation*. This stage presents the full expression of what you are now living without. It brings the feelings associated with great loss. When Mark died, I was full of sadness, *and* I was full of anger . . . at the cancer, at the medical system, at God for taking such a precious life. I was furious. I said to my close, safe friends, "I am whining again today, I am sorry." And they just kept telling me it was understandable. They would be whining too. It was OK. And my anger remained for a few months until it turned to deep sadness and daily cries. My anger was working its way out with safe, listening friends and family. I was walking through the stages of grieving.

Anger may be a messenger that you want what someone else has or is doing. If you are angered by your husband for taking time to play golf or work out, try doing something similar for yourself to see if your anger dissipates. It usually does, because your soul knows you need some exercise and time away too. If a friend is talking about all the wonderful vacations they take, and you find yourself resentful (another form of anger), check out whether that is something you want to do. Probably so! When is the last time you intentionally took time and money for a vacation? You may sound like a victim: *I just cannot get away from all my work. We do not have enough money to take a nice trip. Life is too hard right now to enjoy myself.* Or you can figure out what your resentment and anger are telling you and *do* something about it.

Find healthy ways to off-load this normal, natural response to difficult situations. Why? Because you want to be heard; your anger is a messenger! When you are brimming over with anger, it is nearly impossible for someone to stay there and listen to you. Ask yourself how you do around extremely angry people. I doubt you like to spend time with them. By off-loading some of this emotion in other healthy ways, you are more capable of taking your needs about this emotion to another person and being heard.

How do you off-load anger? You have probably heard some of the ideas below numerous times, and some are creative ideas from women I have counseled. Notice how your feelings may calm down when you work on inviting them outside of you through one of these experiences.

1. Journaling your thoughts and feelings is an easy way to express outwardly what is going on inside you. It does not need to be organized or neat, it just needs to be in writing (or typing).

2. Creating a collage with pictures of what you are thinking and feeling is another good outward expression. One of my clients, who speaks several languages, does this and adds words in multiple languages all around her collage. It is a beautiful way of using her artistic talents to off-load emotions.

3. Talking to someone is one of the quickest ways to off-load your feelings. This requires someone safe, meaning they are not going to give you advice, judge you, spiritualize your situation, minimize your feelings, or break your confidentiality by telling others. If you do this, you will also notice how it grows a closer relationship.

4. Working out or exercising is another way to off-load excessive feelings. I took my anger to a Pilates class one day, where we worked on our core muscles. At the end of the hour, I was astounded that my anger was lessened and more manageable to think about and respond to.

5. Throwing things or other similar physical actions can also be very effective.

A. Egg throwing may sound strange to you, but in my years of working with women and their anger, I have seen it lift the intensity of anger. There is something healing about throwing or hitting something when you are mad. The problem is you do not want to damage things that are valuable or hurt people. Throwing eggs is not only environmentally safe but it lets you get appropriately physical with your anger! Take a carton (or more) of eggs to the woods, and with a permanent marker, write something that is very angering on an egg. Then throw the egg at a tree, announcing the indiscretion aloud. Having a witness contributes to an even more powerful experience. You can take turns speaking and throwing. One client who had been betrayed over many years would report to me, "It was a forty-five-egg day!" She kept a carton of eggs under her bed so whenever her peace was disturbed, she could immediately pull out an egg and write on it for her next throwing. It worked to dissipate that overwhelming emotion inside her so she could access her needs.

B. Another client and her husband sold their house to eliminate triggers from his sexual acting out. They ordered a dumpster before packing. She came to group one day reporting that she was working out her anger as she threw stuff into the dumpster. This petite woman described taking heavy boxes or pieces of furniture and heaving them over the edge while declaring her anger and claiming her needs. She had the privilege of cleaning up and yelling out an overload of emotions that had built up inside her.

C. The privacy of the woods seems to offer many creative ideas to off-load anger. If you do not like the messiness of throwing eggs, banging a whiffle bat on a tree can work to get out some of those emotions. Or maybe you like cutting down trees (if it is your property) or clearing out a densely overgrown area. There are many ways to be physical in nature, connecting your feelings to your behavior to off-load them a bit.

D. I worked with a young mom who was home with her little ones each day. During nap time one day, her anger was overpowering her, so she went into the garage for some privacy. She saw a tub full of children's boots there. She immediately grabbed a boot and hurled it at the wall. Then she smiled and grabbed another. And another. When she reached the bottom of the tub, she collapsed on the floor and released the pent-up anger and sadness that had accumulated.

6. Being alone in the car can also be effective. I talk to many women who love the privacy of their car. I would be among them! A car is a place where, when you are alone, you can talk, laugh, cry, sing, or scream. These all work to off-load emotions.

When you practice off-loading your anger and figuring out what you need, it will be easier to stay current with your anger. That way, when something angers you, it is about the present—not something that happened a month ago, a year ago, or ten years ago. Staying current with anger keeps it from growing too large. When you do not deal with angering situations or take care of needs you have, anger does not just go away. It festers and grows, just like weeds in a garden. You know when you are around someone who has let the weeds of anger grow. You hear complaining, blaming, negativity, bitterness—you hear the voice of a victim.

101

Finally, since anger is a messenger, figure out what unmet needs you have. Your needs may be big or small. You may need time away from children. You may need a more organized house. You may need to reduce your work hours. You may need to have more fun. You may need a new hobby, a new friend, a vacation, or more time to exercise. I called a friend to see if we could get together, and she said, "I have nothing but time today!" Just hearing this helped me identify a desire I had: more unscheduled time. Figuring out what you need is essential for you to take charge of your life and not become a victim. When you are a victim, other people will be the problem. Other people will have to change before you can feel safe and joyful. Other people cause your feelings and, therefore, are intricately involved in changing them. There are no choices besides letting others determine your happiness.

Figuring out what you need and that you have choices in getting those needs met will begin to free you from being a victim and help you move toward living in peace.

You are an intricately designed human being. Becoming a gentle observer to explore yourself is hard *and* life-giving work. What is your worth? Do you have the courage to be imperfect? Do you know what you believe? How is your brain health? How big are your emotions? These are only a few of the components to exploring yourself. They are practical pieces you can work on to become the best version of yourself—the person God called you to be. Please be gentle with yourself and this process. This is a lifelong work, as no one is complete this side of heaven. Life on earth is the dress rehearsal, and you get the opportunity to keep practicing and changing those character traits and beliefs that prevent you from being all God wants you to be. Trials, trauma, and troubles open the door to this journey of self-exploration.

Solving those problems that create pain can become the end of the journey for some. But trauma is not caused by the event itself.

It is caused by what you believe about the event. Real joy comes from moving beyond behavioral solutions. Real joy comes from living with truthful beliefs, changing your character to become more Christlike, and finding your unique passion and purpose for life.

> ▶ Turn to the Gentle Assignments section on page 174 for further reflection.

7

What Is It Like to Be in Relationship with You?

For one human being to love another; that is perhaps the most difficult of all our tasks, the ultimate, the last test and proof, the work for which all other work is but preparation.

Rainer Maria Rilke

I USED TO PLAY ON A TENNIS TEAM. I loved having the companionship of other women and a coach teaching us how to be better players. We spent hours practicing different shots and running through drills. In practice, I felt confident about my skills. But when I was first called into matches with other teams, it was surprising how my skills fell apart when I had the added dimension of a relationship—my opponent! Everything changed. It was evident that learning to be a good player in competition was another level of growth I had not acquired yet. It took years of playing competitive tennis—or I might say *relational* tennis—to get better.

105

And so it will be with emotional and spiritual growth. It will look different when you are practicing with people rather than attending workshops or reading books. God will use your relationships to keep growing you up—if you desire. In relationships you get to practice talking about what you like or do not like about others; getting your needs met while being mindful of others' needs as well; resolving conflict about time, money, parenting, sex, and other important topics; and deciding how you will behave. It is much more complicated. It is not all about you anymore.

The most difficult relationship in which to develop healthy skills will be with your spouse. Your life partner is the most important person in your life, and therefore you have the most to lose if you do not do this well. You sometimes hide away real parts of yourself to keep the peace. You sacrifice being fully known or vulnerable. There may be an unspoken rule that one of you is more important than the other, and sacrifice or surrender is expected. The essence of growing close in relationship is to be fully yourself and to be valued and loved for who you are. When you start straying from living that way, you lose parts of who you are, which can lead to unhappiness or depression. It is a tricky balance to be healthily engaged in a relationship and healthily engaged in your own life.

Most importantly, I want you to hear that no matter how you act in a relationship, your behaviors are not responsible for decisions another person makes about their behaviors. You do not *make* anyone do anything. We all have choices. If someone is disappointed, resentful, or unhappy with you, they can choose to do something about that. No one needs to choose unhealthy or unfaithful behaviors to manage a difficult situation. We are all responsible for ourselves. Let me say it one more time, because I want to make sure you hear it: if you choose to work on changing something about how you live, it is not because you caused your spouse or anyone else to choose their unwanted behavior. It is because you are invested in becoming the person God created you to be. Period.

If you choose to look at who you are in a relationship, especially your primary relationship with your spouse, it will be because you are working on being the best version of yourself. As you make these changes, you will like yourself better, even love yourself. Maybe you will even begin to accept—I mean really accept—the truth of who you were created to be. Fearfully and wonderfully made. Cherished. Unique. Loved. Filled with passion and purpose. No matter what decisions are made for a relationship, you always have this opportunity to work on you. It is often true that when both partners are working on themselves this way, they become safer, more patient, more loving, more vulnerable, more empathetic, and more forgiving. In that place, a relationship can grow and thrive.

Relationships can be fantastic when they are working well and disheartening when they are not. You can sometimes feel cherished and safe and other times used and rejected. If you are not careful, you can quickly decide you married the wrong person. What if God intended for your relationship to keep growing you up and that there would be struggles to work through to do so? What if he knows you have more to learn about becoming Christlike and that your marriage could be the perfect relationship to bring you those opportunities? Our movies about falling in love and living happily ever after have created many false expectations for marriage. A great marriage takes a lot of work, consistent with anything you value.

I noticed that couples engaging in counseling often start by wanting to change each other. "If he would be faithful to me, I wouldn't be so angry." "If she would stop trying to control me, I wouldn't act out sexually." "He's the problem!" "She's the problem!" And on it can go, until the conversation is redirected. The focus in our practice is to encourage each spouse to examine their own life and decide what kind of person they want to be in the relationship. This takes help. Lots of help. We suggest that individual change is possible through a counseling relationship, a group of people who have the same vision of working on themselves, and spiritual direction. When two people are working on changing how they participate in their marriage, the relationship can experience far greater emotional and spiritual intimacy than ever before. It can grow to become a new relationship.

▶ Turn to the Gentle Assignments section on page 176 for further reflection.

8

Practical Steps to Examine Your Relationship

Love does not grow old. It does not age as we do. It develops. And in doing so, develops us.

Leigh Standley

MARK AND I COINED THE TERM *VACUUM THEORY*. This means that if one person in the relationship will not examine their life and own their behaviors, it creates a vacuum or suction that pulls the other person in to start criticizing and suggesting changes. Both partners may participate in this "you're the problem" dynamic if neither owns their own stuff.

Put on your gentle observer cap before you answer this question: *What is it like to live with me?* Give yourself a lot of grace if you are aware that you want to work on changing something. No one does relationship perfectly. The fact that it takes a lot of work to do relationship well is probably why the divorce rate is so high. Not many people are willing to put in that work. We do not just fall in love and live happily ever after. So, remember as you read: grace abounds.

Ask Yourself: How Safe Am I?

I have two stuffed animals in my office that remind me of the person I want to be—and do not want to be. One is a lamb. The other is a porcupine. When my life is going smoothly, it is easy to be "lambish." I can be gentle, kind, soft-spoken, patient, and easy to approach. I do not mean I am without a voice and have no words to speak. Lambs can be noticeably vocal! My problem arises when life is difficult or I have been hurt, misjudged, or betrayed. Then it is easy for me to become "porcupinish." I can be prickly, short, threatening, harsh, and standoffish. I do not mean I should not have righteous anger or disappointment. It comes down to how I display it, what I sound like, and if I am moving toward my understandable need *to be heard.*

Anytime I encounter a porcupine, I move away as quickly as I can. I do not want anything to do with that guy! On the other hand, lambs compel me to move closer, to want to pet their soft fur and share life a bit with them. It is good to be intentional about who we want to be—in all situations. One of my favorite Scriptures is Philippians 4:5, which says, "Let your gentleness be evident to all."

Growing close in any relationship requires you to be a safe person. Even as you walk closer to someone, you are aware of how vulnerable you are the closer you get. You intuitively know you will create distance if that person is not safe. *Safe* can mean different things to different people. Safety for me includes someone who will respect my body and not hurt me or force me to do anything against my will. It includes calm talking and attentive listening. It might also include safe, nonsexual touch, like a hand on my shoulder or a hug. It includes someone who will respect my needs, like wanting to end the conversation or getting help to talk through something difficult.

Your perceptions for safety may include other things. All of us grew up with both elements of safety and relationships that lacked safety. You may have gotten accustomed to people yelling or shouting profanity or barging into your room without permission. You may have witnessed a calm household with little conflict and little interaction. Whatever it was, it contributed to how you sense safety today.

How safe do you feel in the relationship? That is the million-dollar question if you want to grow closer to someone. It is impossible to increase emotional and physical intimacy in a relationship if there is not safety—for both of you. Both partners need to work on being safe verbally, physically, sexually, spiritually, and financially. Those are a lot of components, and it may take work and training to become safer in each. No one is perfectly safe. We all have ways to get better at this.

Practice Do-Overs

No one does life perfectly. Even those who have worked hard to be emotionally healthy will have days that do not go well. Besides getting better at owning when you hurt others, you have the opportunity of cleaning up messy situations after the fact. I call these "do-overs." Have you ever thought about asking someone for a do-over for a conversation or action that did not go well? I think you will find that, in most instances, the offended person will agree.

You can start by naming the situation that went awry. "When you were telling me about your difficult day with some of your colleagues, I immediately started giving you advice and tried to fix it for you. I just want to say I am sorry for not hearing your frustration and disappointment with people you work with. I can imagine that, when that happens, it makes going to work difficult." That is a do-over. It is short, to the point, and owns and corrects what you said or did.

Do-overs are such a gift. When you make mistakes—and you will—you can redeem them. How do you do with redeeming awkward, hurtful situations?

Check Out Your Perceptions

If you are living and breathing, you are assessing things around you all the time. You are making meanings out of what is going on and what you are perceiving. At our counseling center, we ask the question, What is the story in your head? This language indicates that while you are formulating what you think about what is going on, it may, in fact, not be the truth. Learning how to share the story in your head is a healthy component to being in relationship. If you do not, you either assume that the other person just knows what you are thinking, or you may live with inaccurate perceptions yourself. Remember, none of us are mind readers! Even if you have lived in a relationship for a long time, you are still not qualified to read the other person's mind. Inaccurate beliefs or perceptions can lead to a lot of pain, arguments, and disconnection in your relationships.

If you are not invited to a neighborhood gathering, the story in your head may be that you offended someone, and they are excluding you. What may be true is that your invitation was simply lost or forgotten. Your husband may be especially quiet after dinner, and you assume he does not want to be with you. The truth may be that he was removed from a special project at work and feels a lot of shame and disappointment. Your son does not want to introduce you to his girlfriend, so you believe he is ashamed of you. The truth may be that he does not want her to think he is getting serious about the relationship yet.

Learning how to check out your perceptions, meanings, or beliefs—the stories in your head—leads to safer, calmer relationships. When you live in truth, life flows with more peace. Practice sharing a few of the stories in your head and check out whether they are true. Here is an example: "I wanted to ask you to help me with something, but the story in my head was that you were too busy. Is that right?" Or: "When you didn't eat much of the dinner I cooked, the story in my head was that you didn't like what I made. Was that true?"

Ask Yourself: How Do I Handle Conflict?

In a marital relationship, you need to practice balancing your needs (expectations) and his needs, your time and his time, your patterns of living and his patterns of living. It will be a merging of two different lives. In our book *Seven Desires*, Mark and I discuss the desires you will have of each other when you marry. You will have desires for him to hear and understand you, affirm you, value you, keep you safe, initiate safe touch, choose you, and include you.[1] He will have the same desires of you. As much as it seems you are alike in every way when you first meet and initially are faithfully serving each other in all these desires, the infatuation of those first months of a relationship will end. And when it ends and your committed, long-term relationship begins, differences will emerge. He may like to stay up late, and you may like to go to bed early. His sexual interest is not as high as yours is, or vice versa. You love socializing with many people, and he likes small, intimate gatherings. You like an organized environment, and he is rather messy. The differences will show up everywhere. You both might begin to wonder if you married the right person. You will also notice that he is not the perfect spouse you thought he would be—and he will notice the same about you. Disappointment will set in. Conflict will too.

If you are going to grow in your relationship, you will need to be able to resolve conflict. I prefer the term *difference resolution*. What you are facing is a difference of needs or desires. Instead of the idea you're "warring" over these differences, you can acknowledge that differences are normal and expected as you merge two different people from two different environments. The challenge is how you go about managing your merger. Some people choose not to engage at all, and say, "We never fight." While that may sound calm and safe, it does not suggest that a resolution has been reached. Someone must be getting their way, but how was that determined? And what happens to you if it is not you? Do you stuff your emotions and needs or take them elsewhere and secretly get them met? There are many possibilities.

Some couples literally go to war with each other over their differences. There can be yelling, demanding, belittling, shouting profanities, or whatever it takes to "win." Sometimes the winner is predetermined, if the marital pattern has identified the power to be with one or the other. Set aside an hour this weekend to talk with your spouse about what your response is to differences in your relationship. Remember to talk about your response, not your partner's! What do *you* do? Is it healthy? Where did you learn to respond this way? Do you want to work on changing your part? That is something you can do. You will face conflict and differences in all relationships in your life. Getting well and thriving means you will learn how to talk about them and find resolution.

Consider the Turtle and the Hammer

I also have a turtle puppet sitting on my shelf in my office, and a big red hammer is beside it. My turtle and hammer have become symbols of what I often see in marriages. One spouse tends to pursue, pursue, pursue—with questions, ideas, needs, or talking—and the other one retreats and withdraws. You probably get the idea. Turtle draws its head into its shell and will not come out. Hammer sits on top of the shell and pounds away. Unfortunately, the more Hammer pounds, the longer Turtle stays settled inside. Does this feel familiar to you? Which one are you? If this describes your marriage, your relationship will not thrive if things do not change.

Your part is to change what *you* are doing. If you are Turtle, you want to make sure it is safe before you come out to connect. If emotions are out of control or there is no chance to be heard, you decide it is prudent to remain in a safe spot. Ask yourself what you need to come out, because living alone inside your shell is not thriving. It is lonely. Perhaps you need no yelling, no blaming, no pressure to talk, no advice-giving, no threats, no shaming statements about your character, a time limit for how long you will talk—to name a few possibilities. It will be progress to think about what you need and to talk to your spouse about your needs. It might be that he is willing to honor them, or at least work at changing the pattern. And you could practice staying out of your shell until it no longer feels safe, knowing you have a place to go when your feelings shift. Fear and anxiety drive Turtle to choose withdrawal.

It may be that you are Hammer. Hammer uses lots of words, has lots of ideas, asks lots of questions, and has endless initiation for getting her spouse to come out so she can figure him out! It is most likely that Hammer has a desire for more connection, which is an honorable desire. How this desire for connection is being pursued, however, is not working. If you are Hammer, think about ways you feel unsafe to your Turtle partner. How do you express emotions, and how big do they get? What words do you use, and could they be pressuring or threatening? Do you take control of the situation or your agenda with your "helpfulness" and not consider whether your Turtle even wants it? Fear and anxiety drive Hammer to pound. "Will Turtle ever come out? I long for more connection." You may need to hear Turtle commit to talking at some time, perhaps with help to keep things safe.

Both Turtle and Hammer have identical emotions: fear and anxiety. They choose different ways to cope or manage those emotions. And they have the same desire: to be connected. Neither is more problematic than the other. The habits of both lead to distancing in the relationship and the belief that you are not loved by your spouse. Pause your reading for a few minutes and consider whether you might be Turtle or Hammer in your relationship. If you identify with either, ask yourself who might have modeled this behavior when you were young. Then write down your needs as Turtle or Hammer and commit to talking about them with your spouse when things are calm. Ask your spouse if he will do the same for you. Talking about this pattern is the first step to changing it.

Take Ownership

Do you apologize for your missteps? Do you take ownership of your behavior? As Christians, we are directed to look at our own faults (Matt 7:3). Yet, it seems to be easier to blame others rather than admit our mistakes. It feels safer. It is more vulnerable to admit something and own that we are at fault. "I am sorry I did not tell you about having to go out of town this week." "I covered up how much money I spent on the furniture." "I have been critical with you when I know I am bothered by some stuff at work." "I have been worried, and I have not shared my thoughts with you." "I have been lying about where I was. I am sorry."

Owning is spiritual growth. It creates relational growth too. It is unnatural to tell on yourself. When you have hurt others, owning your actions is a way of validating the pain you have caused another person. I do not know of anyone who does not appreciate receiving such ownership from another. It is important, when you are owning your faults, to commit to working to change them. Your ownership is only empty words if you do not change your behaviors. People are more interested in your walk than your talk. You are called to *do* what is right, not just talk about it.

You may not have received any mentoring on owning your behavior as an adult. It is not what you are used to doing. When I ask women what they learned about owning or apologizing from watching what their parents did, most say they did not hear their parents owning anything. Their experience was primarily being told as a child to confess their wrongdoings, or they learned to blame others as they heard their parents doing.

It is also possible that you own too much. You are constantly saying you are sorry for something, even when it is not your fault. You may have learned this as a way to keep the peace with certain people. Maybe you were blamed and criticized excessively as a child, and apologizing minimized the emotional abuse you received. You may have been instructed: Confess. Confess. Confess. While it's important to own what belongs to you, it is equally important not to own what does not. You are not responsible for hurtful behaviors that belong to someone else.

As you are assessing ownership in your relationship, determine what you believe about your own apologies. Too much? Too little? Think about your spouse's ability to own. You may find you are regularly triggered when you expect to hear ownership statements from him but do not. Notice what you do when that happens. Notice what you say. I talked with Connie recently. She realized that lack of ownership on her husband's part led to an instant rageful reaction from her. As we talked about it, she also shared that no adults in her early life owned anything—they only blamed others and blamed her. No wonder there was so much pain behind her response. She also admitted that she did not do a good job of owning, either. She chose to begin working on what *she* could do differently.

Remember to be gentle with yourself as you grow in this area.

Ask Yourself: Am I a Partner or a Parent?

Have you slipped into a parenting role with your spouse? The motivation for being in a parenting role is to help someone improve or correct how they are living or to help them in some way. You may think that if your spouse changes, then you will be happier too. This can involve overdoing for him, offering many great ideas, finding help you think he needs, criticizing him, nagging him, or controlling him. While this may feel helpful to him at first, eventually it will not be received well.

Trying to be a parent to an adult creates a parent-child dynamic that is not intended for a marriage. You are called to be partners, not parents to one another. Such parenting is not the same as *serving* each other in marriage. In healthy marriages, partners do kind things for each other and help with life when it gets stressful. What I am talking about here is a constant pattern of one adult taking over adult responsibilities for the other and creating dependency. Moreover, any adult treated as a child will get angry. Maybe we do not say so, but inwardly it is true. We all long to be an adult and to be able to manage our own life.

Erik Erikson, a renowned psychologist, developed eight stages of psychosocial development from infancy to adulthood (see appendix B). Each stage represents a challenge for the developing psychological needs of the individual. When accomplished successfully, there is a positive outcome for the independence and growth of the person. And conversely, when the stage is not accomplished, there are negative outcomes for their life and an inability to accomplish next stages of growth.[2]

Erikson's second stage, "Autonomy vs. Shame," occurs between the ages of eighteen months and three years, when toddlers are learning to do things for themselves. If you have children this age, you likely hear them demand, "I do it!" or "Me want to do that!" You witness tantrums when they do not get to try things their way. Notice how important it is for a toddler to acquire age-appropriate autonomy. When this stage is experienced in a successful way, children develop a sense of personal control over physical skills and a sense of independence. It leads to confidence in their ability to survive in the world.

When children are criticized or overly controlled in this stage, or others are regularly doing for them what they want to try, they begin to feel inadequate. They can become dependent upon others, lack self-esteem, and feel a sense of shame or doubt about their abilities.

Some of us, in our growing-up experiences, were treated as a child for too long. Parents who cannot let go and let their children make mistakes or fear too many consequences for their children can parent too long in too many ways. We call these "helicopter parents." They hover. They keep making decisions for their children long after it is good for their development. This does not give a child a chance to grow up and practice being an adult before they are one. They stay dependent one way or another on someone else to do adult things for them because that is familiar.

On the other hand, someone may experience an absence of parenting because their parents, in one way or another, were not available. In this situation, a child does not learn some of those skills appropriate for their age, and they eventually turn to others and depend on receiving help from them. In your marriage, you can continue such a pattern. It takes two to create a pattern, by the way. Have you become part of this pattern?

Many people struggle with ADD or ADHD (Attention Deficit Disorder / Attention Deficit Hyperactivity Disorder), which presents problems with focus, follow-through, impulsiveness, details, and organization. Interestingly, these folks may marry someone who is extraordinarily good at getting things done and "cleaning up" after their mistakes. This new partner may take on extra roles to keep things functioning well in the relationship. Eventually, this can lead to resentment or too much caregiving or parenting of another person. Usually, there is not much talking about the source of this pattern. There is just fighting about the unbalanced roles in the relationship or anger at not being a grown-up in an adult relationship.

Have you fallen into a pattern of parenting your partner? Or have you remained too dependent in some area of life and are being parented by your spouse? Please know that I am not talking about loving and serving each other with your strengths. Every relationship that thrives allows two people with gifts and talents to merge those assets. I am talking about a pattern where adults do not fully take adult responsibility for themselves. You will probably know because resentment is growing. Or you might be thinking, *I do all the work around here.* Or you sense you are the one with all the great ideas or initiation. This is not a sign of thriving.

It takes two to continue a pattern of parenting another person: one who receives and one who continues to give. Both have the power to change the pattern. I call it *compassionate detachment* when you desire to move a little further away and allow another person the space to work on learning an adult skill. That does not mean you cannot be helpful or kind in helping your partner with new skills. To be compassionate means to lovingly let someone claim their adult status. This will also involve having the courage to be imperfect. When we practice new things, we will not do them perfectly—or even very well. And that is all right.

Become a Stand-Alone Person

Remember those early days of infatuation when you were first aware of the strong connection to your future spouse? How wonderful it felt to have someone who could take care of you in a way you thought you could not yourself. Or perhaps he was better at something in which you considered yourself inadequate. You looked to your loved one with amazement and affirmed the skills he had to "know you" and "take care of you." It was sweet, and it felt good. This was happening for both of you, and you cherished these interactions. In the beginning, you had boundless energy to "be there" for your partner. You filled important needs for each other. He depended on you, and you felt loved and worthy. You depended on him, and he felt loved and worthy. As you committed to one another in marriage and continued to "grow up" yourselves, these dependencies may have begun to feel like a burden.

You may have felt smothered by another person's helplessness or dependency. And then it was not sweet anymore.

God knew this about us all along. The unconscious connectors of a new relationship are meant to become disappointing along the way so that we can enter a journey of greater spiritual growth and change some things about ourselves. Most of us do not choose to change things in life until they get too annoying or painful. Maybe that is why God reminds us we will all have troubles in our lives. If you examine your life, you might say that positive change happened from the hard stuff you lived through.

Part of working on a healthy relationship is paradoxical: learning how to be all right without it, if necessary, while still choosing to be in the relationship. It means you could be a stand-alone person if you needed to be, *and* you are choosing it because you want it, not because you need it. In other words, you are not choosing your partner because he is going to take care of something for you, you are choosing him because you love *him*. You hope he is doing the same: choosing you because he loves you, not because you are a good sexual partner or a great cook, or because you will manage all the kids' needs while he grows his career. When you choose a spouse for something other than loving who he is, you begin to objectify him. When a spouse is objectified, he can feel used and begin believing, "You do not love me for who I am; you love me for what I can give you." That does not represent a thriving marriage.

What keeps you in a marriage when you have been betrayed and traumatized? I ask women to list the fears they have if they were to leave the marriage. I hear things like, "I do not know if I could take care of myself financially," or, "I do not think I could parent my children alone," or, "I am terrified to be by myself." After they have identified these fears, I suggest they begin practicing to be a stand-alone woman. Some have gone back to school to complete an education for a career. Some have gotten a job to practice making income for themselves if they have never done so. Some have talked with an attorney to know what their situation would be if they did leave. Some have figured out how to get help from others so that they could feel accomplished at mothering without their spouse's help all the time. Some have gone away alone for a short time to practice what that feels like.

I just talked to Latisha, who went on a vacation by herself. Two friends came for part of the time, then she spent the remainder of the days alone. She surprised herself by enjoying her time away. Historically, she always traveled with her husband. She did not know that she could have a good time in a mountain retreat by herself if she chose to. Her dependence on her husband's presence limited her travel when he was not available. She thought she had no other choice, but she was learning that she did. These next right steps help you with your fears so that if you stay in your marriage, it is for a healthy reason—choosing your husband for who he is, not for what he can give you or do for you.

Embrace Authentic Emotional Intimacy

I hear women talking about wanting their husband to be more emotionally involved in the marriage. That is a valid desire and goal for a thriving relationship. It can be hard when your partner is starting to be honest about these vulnerable parts of himself—his feelings, thoughts, and needs. You may see him more angry, more sad, and more anxious, and you worry if this is progress. The truth is this is the authentic man, and he has been hiding many of his feelings. Can you accept all these parts of who he is? For many women, this is hard. Sometimes he is angry with you. Sometimes his sadness may not look as manly as you would like. Sometimes you wonder who will take care of you if he is that anxious. Many issues may arise when vulnerability and intimacy show up. Are you really ready for this? If you are not, that is understandable. You may have safety concerns to address before this kind of honesty can be shared. Many of your needs may prevent you from wanting to work on emotional intimacy. It is helpful to be honest about your readiness.

Please be a gentle observer of yourself. This can be difficult. Your thoughts may take the form of a both/and statement: "I love having a strong, confident man who seems to always like me, *and* I want to work on emotional intimacy and hear when he is angry with me or scared or sad. I accept that if I am to welcome all of who he is, there are many more dimensions to who he is than I have known."

Accept Handicaps

Relationships are where we experience getting hurt and where we practice growing up emotionally and spiritually. Since we are all human and are fallen, none of us will live life perfectly. Most of us try and want to, *and* only God has the power to be all-loving. It is also true that none of us grew up without some hurt, disappointment, and neglect of things we needed to be "mature and complete" in our spiritual character. We all carry flaws. We do not always act rightly, think purely, or love completely. Self-righteousness may tell us we do everything well. We compare ourselves to others and decide we are better. Self-righteousness or pride is a flaw too.

Some of our flaws come from abuse or neglect that have left huge emotional scars in our lives. We have memories we cannot erase. We have unhealthy yet comforting behaviors we cannot seem to escape. We work at changing things and may make some progress. Depending upon the resources we find and the support we engage with, we may make a lot of progress. And then there can be some remnants of emotional disabilities that remain. We get better, but we do not reach perfection. Can we accept that about others? Especially our spouse and other people who are close to us. Can we forgive the times they are hurtful, not only to themselves but also to us? The first step to even asking that question is perhaps asking, "Can I name the flaws in me that lead me to hurt others and to need to ask for their forgiveness?" If you cannot find any, perhaps that is one of the reasons you find it hard to forgive another person. It is most helpful to experience forgiveness for yourself first so that you know how to offer it to another.

I learned how to withdraw to comfort myself when things got painful. When I was little, my favorite place to withdraw was under my bed—with a few Oreo cookies. I had everything I needed to feel better, at least for a little while. I did not have to talk. It took time for people to find me. Chocolate was always comforting. (It still is today!) And eventually I would come out and life would go on. I have worked hard in counseling to change this behavior in my life. For the most part, I give myself an A— today. *And* there are still times I want to withdraw. I think of when I watch one of my children get hurt and I do not know what to do. I think of how I drove to Chicago many times to visit my failing dad. I think of when Mark died. Some of this was self-care, choosing to be alone to grieve or to resist solving others' problems. Some of it was plain old withdrawing.

I contracted polio when I was three years old. Similar to the coronavirus pandemic of today, polio was contagious, and a vaccine was only newly available at the time. My muscles weakened, and I became unable to walk. After a spinal tap (an emotional trauma that stays with me even today), I was diagnosed with the disease. Thankfully, I recovered without needing to wear braces or live with a shortened leg, as some did. It did affect my ability to run fast or even walk without a limp. Sometimes people ask me if I am limping. It is so subtle I do not even recognize it.

During my elementary school days, we had to run a mile to receive the Presidential Award for fitness. That was nearly impossible for me. Instead of understanding that I had a physical limitation that was not my fault, I turned it into shame. *I am not as good as the others. I must be flawed.* I hid from such kinds of activities. I judged myself as incapable. When I think back to my little girl trying to live with a physical disability, I am sad for her. She was doing the best she could. She would never run as well as others who had not faced that trauma. I have learned today that there are many things I love to do, and can do, that are physical. I love golf, tennis, walking, and home improvement projects. *And* I will never be a marathon runner. That is all right.

So, I remember these physical limitations when I'm trying to understand emotional limitations. Some of us will have more difficulty making perfect emotional choices because of long-term woundedness. *And* we all can make enormous progress in much of it. In your relationships, can you improve your acceptance of others who will not do life exactly as you do? Maybe they just cannot. Maybe their life experiences left them with disabilities that are different from yours. We all have one or two "thorns" that God has left in our lives. How are you doing at accepting physical and emotional handicaps in your relationships?

Work toward Unconditional Love

Do you know that one of our greatest fears is being alone? Think about it for yourself. We all do things to be acceptable to others because we do not want to be alone in this world. And when we get close to someone, we're taking the risk that we will be known and rejected.

We all have stories of rejection. Being rejected by a spouse can be extremely painful and adds to that historical pain. It can be difficult to want to "put yourself out there" or be "fully known" when you carry such pain. The risk presents us with a dilemma: *If I choose not to be fully known, then I will not grow as emotionally close in my relationship; if I choose to be fully known, I risk rejection and the possible pain that brings.*

Can you share all your flaws and still be loved? That is unconditional love. It is an awesome goal in relationship, yet no one will ever do it perfectly. Nor will anyone other than God love us that way. We are human beings, and we will fall short. We can keep trying and perfecting how we try to love unconditionally, because I believe that is what Jesus is calling us to do. And by the way, if we only love when another person is very lovable, we will not really know how we are doing at this important spiritual characteristic. We will only get a chance to love someone unconditionally when they are showing us some flaws.

———————

May you become a gentle observer of yourself in relationship, especially your marriage. In a perfect world, that is the closest relationship you experience. Every relationship needs improvement. Could it be that if you are willing to explore some of these dimensions of relationship and work on changing how you show up in the relationship, you will be working on some very practical, spiritual components of love? The one I think is most important is surrendering the notion of living with a perfect spouse! If you learn to do that (and I do *not* mean accepting abusive or neglectful situations), perhaps your spouse will learn to do the same for you. No one is perfect. We all long to have people stay in our lives and love us, even when we let them know who we really are.

> ▶ Turn to the Gentle Assignments section on page 176 for further reflection.

9

A New Trust

Learning to trust will be for all of us the means by which the root system grows firm and nourishes the tree of life.

Elaine M. Prevallet

HAVING YOUR TRUST BROKEN IS PAINFUL. And if trust is broken in your closest relationship, by your spouse, the pain is excruciating. It shatters multiple beliefs you have about yourself, your partner, and your future. It upsets your entire existence. No wonder you may believe nothing good comes out of broken trust.

No one goes through life without trust being broken in some way or another. Perhaps your dad always told you he loved you, but then he started hurting you when he was drinking. Your mom told her friends regularly what a great kid you were, yet her criticism of you never stopped. Your best friend in elementary school dumped you for a new girl who moved in. Your first boyfriend cheated on you with your best friend. Your brother's friends sexually abused you in your home when your parents were away. Your coach sat you on the bench most of the season even though you

were an exceptional athlete. You did not get the job you inter-
viewed for even though you were told you were the best candidate.

When people are dependable—trustworthy—they do what they
say they are going to do, and they offer you some guarantees. "I
can rely on you." "I can be more vulnerable with you because I
know you will not hurt me." "I can feel safe around you." "I can
be myself and know that is good enough for you." "I know you
have my best interest in mind."

Trust is a big word. It carries huge expectations from people,
particularly about safety. We might be thinking, *If I can trust
you 100 percent of the time, then I can finally feel safe.* That
is a lot of trust! Feeling safe is one of the deepest desires we all
have. Remember that safety can be about many things: food,
shelter, money, good health, kind people around you, and, most
importantly, not being alone. When you love someone and they
love you, you want to feel secure and safe. As you think about
trusting another person, you see if they have a good character
and will always care for you, protect you, fight for you, and want
what is best for you. You feel as if you will never have to worry
or feel unsafe again as long as you have your trustworthy person
beside you. It is simple. It is implicit. Love equals trust, and that
equals safety.

When I met Mark and fell in love, I immediately trusted him
completely. He was a pastor's son, he was handsome, he was smart,
he had vision, and he loved me—what more did I need to trust
him? I was only eighteen and never even considered *not* trusting
him. Life was simple then. My trust was uncomplicated. I had a
lot to learn about trusting in a more mature way.

As our marriage unfolded, there were years of secrets and lying
that led to the trauma in our lives. When his secret life of sexual
addiction was discovered, Mark lost his job, his reputation, his
ordination status, his career, and almost his family. I lost a lot too:
my sense of safety, the person I thought Mark was, memories of
what I thought life was, and most of all, my trust. That implicit

trust was crushed, and at first I wondered if it could ever be restored. Over time I found that it was not just recovered as it had been but redeemed with greater complexity. The new trust I have today is something I take into all relationships and situations. It serves me well. It provides safety while still allowing me to be vulnerable, not just walled off from people and life.

Let's take a closer look at building this new kind of trust, one that is more complicated than implicit trust. We'll explore three areas. The first concerns assessing the trustworthiness of another person. The second explores learning to trust yourself. And the third is practicing trusting God; I mean, really trusting him. Since many reading this may be healing from relational betrayal, I'll make some specific suggestions in learning to trust your spouse again.

Trusting Others

We are all imperfect people, and we will fall short of others' need for us to be trustworthy. No one can guarantee how they will live or what they can give you. Anyone can have good intentions *and* also be tempted and fail and fall. When you have been hurt by betrayal, you want a guarantee. Guarantees provide safety so you do not have to worry or get triggered or be scared. I wish you could have a guarantee from a human being, but only God is 100 percent trustworthy. Only he gives guarantees we can trust. And yet we can all work at being more trustworthy, and there are ways we can expect others to contribute to being trustworthy people.

Let us take, for example, a situation of broken trust like mine. As I have said before, my husband and I worked through his sexual addiction and my betrayal trauma. Our subsequent counseling was established for treating couples with this dynamic: a man's addiction and his partner's betrayal. (I know my use of gender pronouns is not appropriate for all addictions and betrayals, but I will use them here as they represent the experience and wisdom

I know.) How could I know Mark was working to rebuild trust? How can you know your spouse is also willing to do so?

1. He is broken and remorseful. In my research project and in my counseling practice, I have seen this is the top trust-builder. He has a "changed" heart. He is *internally* motivated to change.

    There is a humility that comes from owning his brokenness. It is visible to those around him. It is believable. His internal motivation comes from a place of wanting to change his life and initiating what he will need to do.

2. He accepts that he has a problem and is willing to get help.

    With the cultural acceptance of pornography, online chat rooms and profiles, emotional connections with others, physical affairs, and so forth, it can be difficult for a spouse to take some of his acting out seriously. "Everyone is doing it" can seem like a truth to many. It takes courage and conviction for him to accept that, for you and your marriage, it is a problem and does not represent the man he wants to be.

3. He is willing to do *whatever it takes* to be faithful and change his life.

    Being sober is a cornerstone to all the change that can follow. Without fidelity, marital issues will always return to that problem. It is imperative to find a good counselor, a safe community of other men who are in recovery, an expert in sexual addiction, a marriage counselor, and sometimes legal help. No excuses—it must be done if a man is going to *all* lengths to change.

4. He establishes boundaries for himself to resist temptation, triggers, or rituals that would lead to unfaithful behaviors.

    When your spouse is working diligently to be safe in a sexually saturated world, he will determine what he will do to eliminate situations that would create too much temptation for staying sober. If you are the one making suggestions for him, it may be that he is not taking his own boundaries seriously enough. They ideally need to come from him.

5. He does not blame you for his behaviors.

We are all responsible for our own choices and behaviors. No one *makes* us do anything. A man who is taking full responsibility for his life will not blame you for his unfaithfulness. He may have been dissatisfied with something in the marriage or in life, or angry at you for something. *And* there are healthy choices for how to deal with that.

6. He shows patience with your questions, anger, and hurt.

It is understandable that you are angry, sad, scared, hopeless, and whatever else you may be feeling when you discover infidelity. Your spouse may want you to move quickly past your feelings or questions and proceed on to the future. He may profess he will never do anything unfaithful again and believe that you should want to move on too. Your emotions are a natural consequence of what has happened, and they need to be shared (unless they have turned abusive). This takes time.

7. He supports your need to get help—money, childcare, household responsibilities.

One way a partner hears your honest pain is by supporting your need to get help too. Just as he is learning that silence is the greatest enemy to his healing, this is true for you as well. Practical support in the form of money and help with children and your daily responsibilities is the best way to support you in doing that.

8. He is willing to talk about his past and *offer* you full disclosure of all sexual experiences from birth to the present. (Recommended with professional help.)

Building trust is never accomplished by you searching for information or asking probing questions to get information. It is only through the process of your spouse's *offering* that you will feel the difference in trying to build trust again. Creating this sharing with you from the beginning of his life will also help you see the development of the addiction, and hopefully, help you build some empathy and understanding that his behaviors are not about you. The process of full disclosure builds a new foundation of truth-telling for a marriage.[1]

9. He is willing to *offer* information regularly about being faithful/sober.

When someone has broken your trust by being unfaithful, you have understandable anxiety about "how it is going." Is he sober? If you ask him about it, you probably feel like you are being a parent. And he probably reacts as if he is being treated like a child. This recommendation is once again an *offering* of information you need in order to build trust that his life is changing. He will check in with you (ideally daily, until your need changes) with information about sobriety. A check-in called FANOS can provide helpful direction for this sharing (see appendix C).[2]

10. He is willing to be honest about all things: where he is going, who he is with, why he is late, and so forth. He is willing to be an "open book" to build trust.

The definition of sobriety at our counseling center is based on the acronym LAMP.[3] He can claim sobriety when there is no Lying, no emotional or physical Affairs, no Masturbation, and no Pornography. Lying is a critical component because betrayed women are hurt by deception as much as they are by sexual behaviors. Building trust is founded on truth-telling about *all* things.

11. He is willing to work on understanding the "why" of his behaviors—the deeper root causes.

    Stopping behaviors without understanding what drove him to do them does not build trust long term. Knowing the "why" helps him look for healthy solutions to legitimate needs. It also helps his spouse see that change too.

12. He initiates talking to you about his feelings, thoughts, and needs.

    As more safety in the relationship and more practice in how to share vulnerable parts of himself are gained, trust grows in experiencing greater connection with him and seeing him as a different person. These are also new ways you experience your relationship, which builds trust and hope.

13. He follows through. He does what he says he is going to do without reminders or prompting from you.

    He is consistent, dependable, and reliable in all areas of his life. This is not necessarily about sexual addiction. It is about being a person of integrity.

This is a long list, and yet there can be other components you think of that build trust too. When I talk to women who have trouble trusting, it is not uncommon for them to say that very few items on my list would describe their spouse's current actions. On the other hand, for couples that start to feel progress in their journey of healing, all the items in this list will be part of a spouse's desire to repair what has been broken.

Most of us have been betrayed by other relationships too, whether it was a best friend, a former boyfriend, a sibling, or our parents. Many items on this list apply to those situations as well: there is godly sorrow, they accept they have a problem and are willing to change, you are not blamed for the hurt caused, there is patience for your questions and conversation about the hurt, they are willing to be honest with you, and they are consistent in doing what they say they will do. Those who have hurt you will want to work on being a trustworthy person.

Trusting Yourself

Trusting yourself is a difficult concept for many to grasp. As a child, you needed to trust others' opinions and decisions. There was much you did not know. That is what we all do when we are little. We all need encouragement to think, feel, and decide for ourselves as we grow older. That will often include falling or failing sometimes. And parents or caring adults have a hard time letting children do that. You may not have had much practice at making decisions or trusting yourself. It can be easy to live with a belief that, even as an adult, other people know better than you do about what is best for you. Trusting yourself can seem very foreign. Here are some components of learning to do this.

1. Acknowledge your feelings and learn what they are telling you about your thoughts, needs, desires, and decisions. Feelings are messengers, relaying some need you have.
2. Learn to slow down and listen to the "holy whispers" within you (intuition, gut feelings, hunches, red flags). While they have always been there ready to guide you, you may have ignored them or talked yourself out of what they were saying.

   You often need to make yourself quiet and still to hear them too. In John 14:16–17, Jesus says, "I will ask the Father, and he will give you another advocate to help you and be with you forever—the Spirit of truth. The world cannot accept him, because it neither sees him nor knows him. But you know him, for he lives with you and will be in you." And his still small whisper sends thoughts that pass through you or feelings you cannot ignore that lead you to do something—your next right step.

3. Know the truth about who you are based on how God defines you, not by how others define you. You are worthy. You are capable. You are beloved.

    Trusting yourself means you will stop looking for approval from others, including your spouse, and learn to receive God's approval and acceptance. It also means who you are is not determined by what your spouse has done.

4. Assess your fears and anxieties and work on healthy ways to eliminate or manage them. It is easy to want a spouse to manage these for you. Ultimately, it is your responsibility to do that.

    Being an adult means you practice doing adult things like taking care of your emotions. This can be unfamiliar when you have been dependent upon your husband or other loved ones to help manage them for you. This is part of practicing being a stand-alone person as I described in chapter 8.

5. Commit to becoming a whole person, capable of being alone if you need to be, so that you are not making decisions out of fear.

    This continues the concept of being fully adult. It does not mean you do not ask for help at times. When you find that you cannot live without someone helping you in some way all the time, that is a sign of dependency.

6. Grow your safe community, identify your needs, and ask for help. You are not dependent on your husband to provide all you need for your life to be all right.

    This idea is hard for some wives. "Why did I even get married?" some would ask. Expecting someone to be there for you in all ways and at all times is an impossible pressure to put on anyone. If you are the recipient of that kind of relationship, you know the smothering you feel from such dependency. Learning to include other safe people in your life frees you up to *choose* your spouse to love, not *need* him to love.

7. Demonstrate that you are trustworthy despite what others are choosing to do. Choose to walk the "high road."

    Learning to be trustworthy yourself in all situations and with all people leads to a sense of integrity and loving yourself. Choose to do the right thing no matter what. "Let us not become weary in doing good, for at the proper time we will reap a harvest if we do not give up" (Gal. 6:9).

8. Examine your life to understand old experiences or messages about trust. When you've had your trust broken previously, it is easy to add that pain onto current incidences of broken trust and hand over all your pain to your current betrayer of trust.

    This is an encouragement to look at your earlier life experiences at home, school, church, neighborhood, work—wherever you may have been betrayed. When you pile up pain from past experiences, it contributes to the current pain you feel. Working on feeling the emotions of those experiences is important to your well-being and to improving your chances to trust more completely today.

When you love someone, it is easy to become dependent upon what that person can do for you and how they take care of you. That is sweet when the relationship is new. *And* it is important not to abandon your job: to become fully an adult, capable of knowing your worth, your value, and your ability to manage your life with God alone should you need to. Can you trust that about yourself?

Trusting God

Many of you have difficult stories that have shattered your trust in God. Trauma can do that. It is understandable, and it is a common story. Perhaps you have never tried to put trust in him and simply do not have stories to confirm it one way or the other. Until God is all you have, you may not have experienced that God is all you need. Another important component of growing may be to experience how your faith develops in these difficult circumstances.

Some of you may be confused about trusting God because religious people in your life have not been trustworthy. They may hold secrets, lead a hypocritical life, or hurt or abuse loved ones, and yet they profess to be a Christian. How can that be? Your mind wonders and holds back trust of this magnificent God who has allowed this incongruent relationship to exist. I have talked to numerous men and women for whom this paradox prevents their spiritual growth. "My dad is a pastor and uses pornography, but he will not admit it is a problem. He says I am the reason my husband has issues with porn." "My youth pastor sexually abused me when I was a teenager, and it really messed with my beliefs about God." "My parents are leaders in our church and are thought of as icons of the community. At home they argue continually and refuse to get help for fear of people finding out their struggles."

Growing your trust in God will lead you to work on the following things.

1. Surrendering your spouse's life to God's protection and care, knowing that you cannot control another person's behavior.

   This does not mean you do not need him to work on being trustworthy or that you never speak up about how you are feeling or what you are thinking. It means you do not take charge and try to control your partner to get him to live rightly.

2. Surrendering your life to God, trusting that he will provide for all your desires and needs, even if your earthly relationships do not. He wants you to totally depend on him. "Take delight in the LORD, and he will give you the desires of your heart" (Ps. 37:4).

   This means accepting that another human being, even your spouse, will not always be able to give you all that you need or want, and God is waiting for you to trust him with that task. It will require going to him to do so and then waiting for his response.

3. Trusting that God's timing (as slow as it seems sometimes) is perfect timing for your healing and growing process.

   This is difficult for most of us, who are busy, rushed, impatient, and planners. You have ideas and are a "get 'er done" person. The thought of taking time when you are hurting is unimaginable. And yet God is calling you to try this out. Wait on his timing. It is always perfect.

4. Trusting that God will provide the information you need to be able to trust, even when you can't seem to get it yourself.

   This can be difficult when you are driven to find evidence to validate your internal "knowing." Again, when you have done what you can, it may be time to surrender to God, who has power to uncover truth in miraculous ways.

5. Shifting the trust that you were blindly giving to your husband—an imperfect human being—to God, your only source for total trust.

   This will involve surrendering your agenda, your timing, and even your hoped-for results to God, who oversees all your life.

6. Trusting that God will never abandon you, although he may seem silent and distant at times.

7. Trusting that God loves you, his precious one, and wants to prosper you and give you life (Jer. 29:11).

8. Figuring out the next right step rather than trying to control your future and figure it all out weeks or months ahead of time.

   "Although the Lord gives you the bread of adversity . . . your ears will hear a voice behind you saying, 'This is the way; walk in it'" (Isa. 30:20–21). Trusting is not just sitting on the couch doing nothing and waiting on God. Trusting is active: you do what you can and then surrender the rest to God to take over.

9. Trusting that God will not waste your pain but will use it to strengthen you personally, relationally, and spiritually (James 1:12).

   Living through trials, trauma, and adversity and eventually experiencing growth is the only path that will confirm this truth.

Mature trust is complicated. Waiting for someone else to do all the right things so you can trust again leaves you dependent upon another human being for the rest of your life—because your trust is built externally. Learning to trust yourself and to trust God, however, creates internal trust. You can take internal trust anywhere. You can use it to take chances, be vulnerable, and grow close to others, knowing you can quickly change course if you need to.

The Spirit within you is a powerful gift to lead you in all situations. In all adversity or traumatic situations, the Spirit will lead you to your next right step if you will listen and act. Your dependence on God's delivery of all you need for today will increase. It is a beautiful relationship of growing your trust in the only trustworthy One—God.

Only you can decide how you will respond to disappointment or deception regarding trust. It is normal to build up walls and shut people out when your trust has been broken. Even God can be ignored. No relationship will give you perfect trust. *And* you will hurt or disappoint others when you are not perfectly trustworthy. We are human. We all fall short of loving and providing safety for each other. Trusting people helps us to feel safer, and thus we grow closer to them. When you are safe, others find you more trusting and desire to grow closer to you. This works with God too. A new way to trust can emerge from trauma.

▶ Turn to the Gentle Assignments section on page 177 for further reflection.

10

Everything Cries Holy—
Letting Life Teach You

We must be ready to allow ourselves to be interrupted by God.

Dietrich Bonhoeffer

INSTEAD OF ASKING GOD, *WHY ME?* I am learning to ask, *What do you want me to learn?* I've worn out a CD, *Come Heal This Land*, of Robin Mark singing "Everything Cries Holy." I have often told clients that everything is information: facing discoveries, having difficult conversations, engaging in full disclosure, speaking up about something important, or making a tough decision. No matter how it goes, it will tell you something about another person—and it will tell you something about yourself. Now I also like to say, "Everything cries holy!" God will use anything in your life to teach you something he wants you to learn. If you have not learned a lesson God believes is important for you to learn, I believe he keeps sending the lesson in other formats or relationships until you notice. He is persistent!

Maybe God wants you to watch the reaction of your spouse or your boss when you learn to ask for your reasonable needs, or you say no to a request that is not congruent with your values. Everything is information. You learn something. God may want you to see that, in many daily interactions, you are not living with a safe person. Maybe you have minimized those reactions, or you are used to them because it is what you saw in your own family growing up. *And* maybe God wants you to live differently, receiving the love and respect you deserve. Pamela finally left a marriage when her husband would not stop using pornography. She quit seeing her dad when he would not stop blaming her for her husband's addiction. She left a job when her boss yelled at her and was constantly critical of her work. I reminded her that lessons were coming to her from all over, and she was finally getting God's message: "I do not want a precious child of mine to be abused."

I counseled Mary, who struggled with her reactive anger. She eventually called it her addiction to rage. I was proud of her for naming something that did not represent the woman she wanted to be. She'd justified the rageful outbursts, which included damaging household items and even breaking her own toe as she kicked the car because she was angry at her husband for his many years of betrayal. She felt entitled to her anger. When she started examining her responses to difficult conversations with her children and at work, she began to see that God was bringing more lessons. She went to work on understanding what drove her impulsive rage. With the help of accountability partners, she began exploring what triggered her prior to her rage and figuring out what needs she had when she was angry, and she slowly changed this ungodly trait to a healthier response. She loves this part of who she is today: a gentler woman who can still talk about her anger and ask for her needs to be met. I am sure God is beaming with pride as well. I would add that her relationships in all arenas of her life have changed too, because she is a safer person.

Perhaps you have noticed that you are not very patient. I counsel Mikala, who said, "I really don't wait well." What an honest confession. As she worked on slowing life down, I could see it was uncomfortable for her. Slowing down is so difficult for so many of us that God gives us ample teachable moments to practice. Or at least the free will he imparts to you allows you to notice some patterns in how you live. Are you running late all the time? Do you find you are using every last minute to squeeze in one more to-do item on your list? Do you multitask regularly? Do you take work with you when your spouse invites you to go on an outing with him? Do you help your children with their homework while talking on the phone? Many of us do not know how to slow down. Many of us do not wait well. God sends multiple opportunities for us to practice, because being patient is important to being "mature and complete." Are you noticing what you are missing when you are moving so fast?

Maybe you express your emotions with great intensity, or they are unregulated. When you are mad, everyone scatters to get away from you. Or when you are sad, you stay in your room for hours at a time. Or when you are happy, your excitement comes spilling from the sky and lands on everyone. "What you see is what you get," said a client to me (and I hear that often). That could sound like someone being authentic. It could also be someone who does not want to own that her out-of-control emotions could be tamed and presented in a healthier, more godly manner. Lessons will keep coming if it is the latter.

"I love to give advice," Maria mentioned in one of my groups. "I feel better if I think I've helped someone." I asked her if others liked her advice. She paused and said, "Well, I do notice they often look frustrated and stop talking. And eventually, they don't share as much with me." We discussed how Maria felt when others gave her unsolicited advice. She began to understand her unsolicited advice was a problem and decided she was going to approach conversations differently. Maria admitted that it was hard, because she realized she had received a lot of advice from her dad, who was an attorney, and her mom, who was a teacher. The pattern was familiar. She recognized that it had created a lot of anger in her as she was growing up, so no wonder others did not like her being an unsolicited advice-giver. Lessons began pouring in once she started noticing.

If you use your current adversity to justify your every trait, you may miss the opportunity to look at longtime patterns you have carried with you. God wants you to be "complete, not lacking anything" (James 1:4). We all have work we could do. Everything around you cries holy if you care to notice. *What do you want me to learn today, God?*

Loneliness versus Solitude

Being quiet will help you "hear" what God wants you to learn today. It will also lead you to your next right step (guidance). For many people, being quiet with no outside distractions can feel uncomfortable and lonely. Henri Nouwen, a writer, professor, and monk, suggested that

> loneliness is one of the most universal sources of human suffering today. . . . The roots of loneliness are very deep and cannot be touched by optimistic advertisement, substitute love images or social togetherness. . . . No friend or lover, no husband or wife, no community or commune will be able to put to rest our deepest cravings for unity and wholeness.[1]

Do you ever drive in your car in silence, without music or sports or talk show hosts discussing news of the day? Do you go for walks and leave your earbuds at home so you can listen for the sounds of nature and for God's voice? When there is no one else in your house, do you leave the TV off and take time to be alone with God? Pay attention to what you do to avoid silence. Silence can feel lonely. In the loneliness, we all look for ways to be distracted and busy so that we do not need to feel alone.

There is a difference between loneliness and solitude, says Nouwen. Solitude is not just about being physically separated from the world, though at times it may be helpful to create that distance. Solitude is a knowing of the heart. It is about experiencing peace within, regardless of the stimuli or situations that surround us. It is about knowing God's truths: *I am with you, I am for you, I will give you all the delights of your heart.* Solitude is a spiritual connection with God. It is knowing you receive all you need from him, and therefore you do not need to cling to others or be dependent for fear of being left alone. When you are living with God, you will never *be* alone. This is different from *feeling* alone. Even naming it differently might help you to embrace the idea and practice it more regularly.

Adversity or suffering can slow down your life enough that you finally face loneliness. Then you have a choice to embrace it and learn what solitude can teach, or you can fill the space back up with "busyness" and "life." In solitude, you connect to the Holy Spirit for guidance in living your life. You can access feelings or passing thoughts that lead you to explore your next steps.

I met with a wife who had newly discovered her husband's secret life of sexually acting out. She was devastated and emotionally exhausted. Her life was packed with raising five children, full-time work, and additional administrative support for her husband's business. I asked what she needed, and she quickly said she did not know. And then she said this: "I just want some space and some peace and quiet. I'm so tired." I asked her what she might do to get a little bit of that right away. She had another immediate response: "I do not want to take care of my husband's billing anymore. He can find someone else to do that!" Though she did not call it the Spirit within her that led to this next right step, I knew it was. I love that about listening for God's direction.

Ahas Are Personal!

If you are a jigsaw puzzle person, you know what it is like to find a piece that has been missing for hours. *Aha—I found it!* I love ahas in the counseling process. They come bursting out when some piece of life comes together with a new understanding. They are like puzzle pieces of your story—the picture of your life. You are filled with adrenaline when you find something that has been missing or land on a truth. These truths are lessons God wants you to learn. Sometimes they are about changing the way you are doing something. Sometimes they are about a belief you hold on to that is not your truth today. Sometimes they are about understanding why you have acted in or felt a certain way. Lessons from God come with ahas. Ahas are small slices of truth. No wonder we feel freer and relieved. They come from within us. No amount of outside advice or information can make them happen if you are not ready to make the connection. They burst forth when *you* connect something about your life story with information. They allow you to understand, shed shame, or be more compassionate to yourself or others. Everything cries holy. When we begin to welcome the lessons, the puzzle pieces start falling into place. The picture becomes recognizable and makes sense.

Here are some ahas from women I have counseled:

- It made sense that I do not trust men when I remembered my grandfather and uncle sexually abused me. I never talked about that or dealt with how painful and confusing that was. I only knew that, in my mind, men were not trustworthy or safe. Aha!
- Of course I struggle with lack of confidence. When I realized how critical my parents and coaches were, it makes total sense. I did not have encouraging people around me. I get that now and hopefully can stop blaming myself for not being more confident. Aha!

- I can see I was surrounded by black-and-white thinking at my church, and I now have trouble accepting that truth can be complicated. Using both/and statements feels good—and awkward! Aha!

- I know I was loved in my family, *and* I also see now that most of the love I received was when I accomplished things and did well. Today, I believe I work and volunteer until I am burned out to keep earning others' love. It is still hard to believe I could be loved just for who I am. Aha!

- I did not realize I had learned to tolerate a lot of intolerable treatment. It became so normal that I accepted it as how people treat each other. Living with my friend's family for a while showed me that conversations can be peaceful and loving, and people can be kind to each other. Aha!

- I have been anxious for a long time, and I am beginning to recognize that. I was bullied in elementary school, and I became fearful of a lot of things. I have never talked about it until now. I lived with those uncomfortable feelings, an inability to sleep well, and hypervigilance about many things. Aha!

- My parents grew up with little financial security. It is no wonder that they are so overly involved in how I spend money. I know now that it is about wanting a better life for me, not about trying to control everything I do. Aha!

When you are committed to a journey of self-examination, you will be filled with ahas along the way. You will be excited to feel like you are growing, becoming "mature . . . not lacking anything" (James 1:4). It is compelling, exciting, *and* hard sometimes to see all that God has for you if you are willing to put in the time and resources to explore.

You will never finish the journey of maturity this side of heaven. There will always be something more you can learn and improve as you seek to be the person God created you to be. This is a lifetime journey, not a short ride following a trial or adversity in your life. Of course, it is your choice whether you step on board. Jessie once said in a counseling session: "I hope I live long enough to grow up!" Her humor reflected a great attitude of accepting that growing up takes more than a couple of months or years. And maturity is more than healing from a traumatic life experience.

Stadium Seating

I've had two opportunities to go watch the Minnesota Vikings, our NFL team in Minneapolis. My first trip was an exciting adventure. Mark and I were given front-row tickets by a friend of the team. We were so close, I felt like I could have grabbed one of the players as they ran by. I could see the expressions on their faces and hear the impact of their tackles. Talk about being in the game! The problem was, I was so close to the action, I could not make sense of what was going on. It was one big pile of people scrambling for a football. All the plays looked about the same to me. It would have been hard for me to decipher what the next best play would be.

The second time we went to a Vikings game, Mark and I took the kids and chose less expensive seats in the upper deck. The seats were so high that we practically touched the Metrodome roof! We were far away from the action, *and* the view gave us an incredible big-picture perspective of what was going on. However, I could not even distinguish the numbers on their jerseys, so watching the game felt rather impersonal.

These two games seem like a perfect analogy of figuring out lessons from God: *What would you have me learn, Lord?* When you are in the middle of something difficult, it is like sitting in the front row. You are in every play, and you are so close to the action it is hard to distinguish what is going on. You can be tempted to make judgments. You might want to get out of there. It is too intense. You would like to understand it all now, while the play is fresh, and make decisions about the future. And that is difficult. When you get further away from your circumstances and the people in them, it becomes easier to make sense of the situation. You can see the bigger picture. You can see what is working and what is not. You are more removed from all the triggering that can happen when you are too close. The top row is a good place to review, revise, and reestablish a plan. It is a good place to take in a lesson. And maybe even have an aha!

When you are moving through traumatic situations or adversity, you start out with front-row seats. No wonder we are generally advised not to make big decisions or changes in life when in crisis. Our front-row seats do not allow for the bigger picture experience that will inform healthy choices. Let the game play out. And then remember, you will need a top-row seat to do the important work of looking at the big picture.

God Won't Waste Your Pain

> Were it possible for us to see further than our knowledge reaches, and yet a little way beyond the outworks of our divining, perhaps we would endure our sadness with greater confidence than our joys. For they are the moments when something new has entered into us, something unknown; our feelings grow mute in shy perplexity, everything in us withdraws, a stillness comes, and the new, which no one knows, stands in the midst of it and is silent.[2]

When you are in the middle of crisis or loss, it may not seem like there is any good at all about what is happening. But Scripture says, "In all things God works for the good of those who love him" (Rom. 8:28). When I think about this verse, I like to add the word *eventually* to the end. "In all things God works for good, eventually."

Eventually might remind you that what looks like a disaster now may, in time, turn out to be quite different. It might suggest that there are "plans to prosper you and not to harm you, plans to give you hope and a future" (Jer. 29:11). They have just not been revealed yet. *Eventually* might be teaching you that God has more ideas and plans than you could ever imagine. He might want you to work through yours first and then turn things over to him to watch the divine power he has. Who knows exactly why things happen or when they happen for good—I just know they do. As I get older, I have the privilege of watching more stories play out. And today, I live assured in the truth that God will not waste your pain—or mine.

When you look at the bigger picture of your story, you may begin to see where good did follow adversity. When you were in the game, in the trial, it appeared to be nothing but a loss. And yet in time . . . eventually . . . growth and good emerged from your situation. Hindsight is often a better teacher than foresight.

Surrender, Surrender, Surrender!

Surrender is a key part in the healing and growth process. Surrender involves both action and trust in God. Surrender does not mean you immediately say, "OK, God, I'm going to sit over here on my couch and wait to see what you are going to do. You know what is best. I trust you've got this for me." Surrender involves action first. Surrender asks you to do what you can do. You are not helpless. You can ask for the Spirit to lead you to what you need to do. You can ask for help. You can also *do* some things to take care of yourself. Surrender happens when you have done all that you know to do, and you are still not getting the results you had hoped for. You want your husband to go to counseling every week, and he is canceling most of his appointments. You want him to be more empathetic about your hurt, and he just walks away when you start sobbing or yelling again. You are frustrated that you are still feeling sad and lonely several months after losing your job. You are angry with God and confused about why he did not protect you from sexual abuse as a little child.

Learning to surrender to God—his timing, his plans, his understanding, his provision—will lead you to greater peace. It will help you identify where your healthy efforts are turning into unhealthy controlling. When you try to control your environment or other people, you begin to feel anxious, frustrated, or resentful. That is when God reminds you that if you want peace in the chaos of life, you need to keep your thoughts on him and your trust in him (Isa. 26:3).

I learned to say to myself, *I will do what I can and then surrender the rest to God.* For me, it makes a significant difference to know I am surrendering to God and not just letting go. Surrendering without God might feel like giving up or giving in. It might seem like I am just accepting defeat. It does not feel very hopeful. When I surrender to God, who is all-powerful, all-knowing, and all-present, it feels like I have invited in the smartest, most experienced, and most resourceful person on earth! I can turn over my desires and efforts to the eternal president of my board of directors! That gives me comfort. That gives me peace. "And the peace of God, which transcends all understanding, will guard your hearts and your minds in Christ Jesus" (Phil. 4:7).

I do not do this surrendering perfectly, *and* it has improved so much over the years. I am grateful that when I am living through the greatest trauma of my life—the death of my spouse—I have learned how to surrender to God. I will do what I can to grieve, to take care of myself, to be with family and friends, to find meaningful work and joy. I will trust his timing, his agenda, his understanding, and his next right step for me.

> Take delight in the LORD,
>> and he will give you the desires of your heart.
> Commit your way to the LORD;
>> trust in him and he will do this:
> He will make your righteous reward shine like the dawn,
>> your vindication like the noonday sun. (Ps. 37:4–6)

I especially like the notes in my Life Application Study Bible for these verses:

> To commit ourselves to the Lord means entrusting everything— our lives, families, jobs, possessions—to his control and guidance. To commit ourselves to the Lord means to trust in him, believing that he can care for us better than we can ourselves. We should be willing to wait patiently for him to work out what is best for us.[3]

In everything, God works to teach us that he wants us to depend on him—for everything. Not depend on yourself. Not depend on your spouse. Not depend on family or friends. Not depend on what you think you need to do to be a good person. This is not to say that loved ones in your life cannot be helpful or available to you. But when they have done all that you have asked or all that they will do and it still is not enough, God says, *Please come to me. I am here for you. Depend on me, oh precious child of mine.*

We admire independence. And it is good to be competent and confident, and to provide for your needs. However, maybe you carry it too far. You not only do not let others in, meaning you do not ask for help or appear to need help, but you continue to depend on yourself for all your needs. And you get burned out, tuned out, and depressed. "It is too much," you say. And it is. God does not want your life to feel like that. He urges you to be in community with others, to share the burdens of life. He also wants you to depend on him for guidance to cut out the stuff that is not that important or to ask for help for what is.

Mary and Martha in the Bible give us a good lesson. When Jesus comes to visit them, Martha attends to all the details to make everything perfect. Mary sits at Jesus's feet, soaking in his words and presence. Martha is so tired from all her doing that she gets irritable and wants Jesus's opinion on all she is doing that Mary is not. "'Martha, Martha,' the Lord answered, 'you are worried and upset about many things, but few things are needed—or indeed only one. Mary has chosen what is better'" (Luke 10:41–42).

I have been a Martha. The lessons keep coming, and I am still working on being a better Mary. I am good at details. I can do a lot of things. I often do not ask for enough help. I often focus too much on what does not matter. God reminds me: *Let it go. Give it to me. Surrender. Everything cries holy.* I am more aware of my dual identity—Martha and Mary. I am learning to welcome details when they are needed without sacrificing a calm presence. I think they can coexist. After all, Mary and Martha were sisters. I would like to think they were twins, like my sister and me.

When we walk through painful times, I believe we are being called to work on two of God's most important commandments. First, "Love the Lord your God with all your heart and with all your soul and with all your mind," and second, "Love [others] as yourself" (Matt. 22:37–39). What if God continues to give us lessons so that we will work on these two commandments? The lessons keep coming. Are you prepared to keep asking, "What do you want me to learn?"

As we work on letting all of life grow us up, toward completion, perhaps we are working on living out one of the components of these commandments:

Loving God
- To delight yourself in him so that he can give you all the desires of your heart (Ps. 37:4).
- To know he is with you and for you always.
- To know he is all-wise, and you have limited understanding and solutions. To surrender when you have done all you know to do.
- To accept that his timing is perfect—and sometimes much slower than yours!
- To trust he wants to continue growing you up.

- To experience his forgiveness and deep love for you when you "own" your sin.
- To depend on him: "I'll never know that God is all I need until God is all I have."

Loving Others

- To be safe—physically, emotionally, spiritually, sexually, and financially.
- To be encouraging and affirming.
- To want what is best for another person.
- To look for the good in another person (Phil. 4:8).
- To be a possibilitarian—to have new filters to understand others rather than judging.
- To give generously to others—time, money, talents, and mentoring.
- To love others despite their inability to love you in return.

Loving Yourself

- To accept that God is the master Creator of all things beautiful—you are worthy, valuable, lovable, and choosable. You do not need to earn this blessing; it accompanied you at conception.
- To know you have been uniquely created with your own gifts and talents. When you are authentic, you connect with your uniqueness.
- To know you have been instilled with a passion and a purpose especially designed for you, to spread love and compassion to others.
- To know God wants you to enjoy the pleasures of his world—to take time, money, and resources for yourself to experience joy—to play.
- To not take yourself too seriously or be too perfectionistic and miss out on connection and relationships with others.

When you face adversity or traumatic life experiences, you come face-to-face with God's most important commandments. How are you doing at loving God, others, and yourself? When you are in pain or afraid or angry, it is understandable to want to control others, control your situation, or find unhealthy coping to manage your pain. You are not your best self. You are distracted from loving God, others, or yourself well. As we talked about in prior chapters, controlling or coping is different from figuring out what you need by listening to the Spirit within you. God will reveal your next right step, sometimes with a thought that floats through your mind, sometimes with a feeling that reminds you of something you need, or sometimes in a conversation with a friend or counselor.

God's direction may come from the small whispers that show up as thoughts in the quiet of a walk, or late at night, or when you're in your POYO. Or they show up as "threads of curiosity," as I call them.[4] Small sparks of joy that show up to lead you to try something different and slowly guide you to more and more joy and peace. Or they show up as emotions begging to be heard and understood. After Mark died, my body begged me to rest and sleep. When I heard that plea, I decided not to schedule anything in the mornings or to set an alarm clock. It has been a year and a half, and I am still listening to the need for more rest. What are the small whispers trying to teach you?

Women say to me, "What if I miss God's direction? What if my feelings or thoughts are not from the Spirit but are just from me trying to control something?" Remember, God is like a GPS. If you miss a turn, the GPS voice redirects you: "Make a U-turn at the next intersection and go this way." If you make a decision that is not taking you in the right direction, God will redirect your path. He knows where he wants you to go. He is the master GPS! And how will you know you've made a wrong turn? You will know because your peace is gone. Peace always follows when we take Spirit-led steps. Isn't it amazing that we have been given this simple way of knowing if we are in God's path? He "will keep in perfect and constant peace the one whose mind is steadfast [that is, committed and focused]" on him (Isa. 26:3 AMP).

I have a conversation with God every morning when I am getting ready for the day. I ask him:

What do you need me to surrender today?

Is there something you want me to learn today?

What will I need your help with today?

What is my next right step for today?

As I have focused on these questions, I find that throughout my day the answers always come. *Aha! There it is!* I smile as I land on his guidance. More than any other spiritual practice, this has kept me close to God and his Spirit.

Everything cries holy. There is always something more to learn.

> Come to me, come to me, O my God;
> Come to me everywhere!
> Let the trees mean thee, and the grassy sod,
> And the water and the air![5]

▶ Turn to the Gentle Assignments section on page 178 for further reflection.

11

Liking the New You—Transforming

Part of the adventure of my life is—I don't know all that I may become.

Martha W. Hickman

EXPLORING YOUR STORY MEANS "TO KNOW." Who are you? What do you believe and why? Why do you do what you do? What formed and shaped you? No matter what the content of your previous chapters has been, your story can lead you to well-being, to healing from adversity, to becoming the person God created you to be. Your story still has chapters to be written. Everything in your life cries holy and begs to be understood in the bigger picture God is writing for you. He is in the upper row of the stadium! You are still down in the game. He knows where he wants to take you. Will you trust him to make you "mature and complete, not lacking anything" (James 1:4)? It is a lifetime journey.

What does maturing look like? How does it show up in your life? The Posttraumatic Growth Inventory (PTGI) identifies specific elements of growth for those who have experienced adversity in life.[1] I used this inventory in my research with over two hundred relationally betrayed women, 96 percent of whom had been "very or extremely traumatized." These women had accessed elements of support through counseling for cognitive restructuring, safe community, full disclosure of truth, and spiritual direction. Even though one-third of the participants had only been in a recovery program for one year or less, all five categories of growth as identified by the PTGI saw at least some to very great change:

Category of Growth	% Change
Changed sense of self	88.7%
Deeper spiritual wisdom	87.0%
Richer relationships	86.2%
Greater appreciation of life	85.3%
New possibilities in one's life	83.5%

The women in my research also took the Intimacy Skills Inventory I created, and they reported growth in these areas:

Category of Growth	% Change
I more easily identify behaviors I need or want to change.	59%
I know I always have choices.	58%
I take responsibility for my own feelings, thoughts, behaviors, and happiness.	58%
I create safety for myself.	58%
I have safe people in my life.	56%
When I make mistakes, I readily own what I do wrong.	56%
My life has significance.	52%
I can see different perspectives. I am not black-and-white about things.	52%
I can allow others to be different than I am.	50%
I have courage to be imperfect.	50%
I like who I am and consider myself worthy.	48%
I am resourceful.	48%

I trust myself.	47%
I state my needs and desires clearly.	45%
I am proactive rather than reactive.	39%
I can enjoy the moment without getting overly focused on the past or the future.	31%
I trust others.	18%

These are tangible elements of change and growth. This is incredibly hopeful! These women had been moving through extreme trauma, and with help and even within a fairly short period of time, they were already experiencing this growth.

Learning new ways to think, believe, and act can lead to new ways of living and relating to others, including God. Looking at the Fruit of the Spirit also provides a good assessment of growth (Gal. 5:22–23).

Are you living with more *love* for yourself, others, and God?

Do you feel more *joy* in your days?

Is there more *peace* in your life?

Do you have more *patience*?

Is there more *kindness* in your actions?

Is there *goodness* in your choices?

Are you *faithful* to God's bigger plan for you and his direction for your life?

Does *gentleness* describe you?

Do you portray *self-control* in your living?

When you are living with more Fruit, you are also making progress in connecting with the passion and purpose God has instilled in you. Your life has meaning. Your story has purpose. You were given specific personality traits and talents to grow your unique life. And when you connect to those threads of curiosity that God is continually planting in your soul, your joy grows, and you feel

159

the live-streaming of the Lord in your life. I am not talking about gigantic ventures or world-changing jobs. I am talking about paying attention to the small threads that birth some interest or talent you have. These threads come from listening for the Spirit within you. It is a nudge, a thought that says, *Why don't you try this? Or initiate that? Or change this decision to one that is more peaceful?* When you connect to that thread, your energy grows, and your heart sings a bit more. And it leads to growth. With every small decision, you trust God is leading you somewhere. You are following, even though you do not know where you will be going. He wants you to feel alive because your life has meaning. Let your story unfold.

If you like the new you, you are liking the qualities of a thriving person versus those of a surviving person. The new you will like thinking about the both/and and love the color gray—a reminder that the truth is a mixture of several beliefs. You will take responsibility for yourself and choose to be intentional about vision for your life. You know you are worthy and your life has meaning, regardless of what others say or do to you. You desire to keep learning from all circumstances, especially the painful ones. You believe growth is possible for everyone if there is commitment to that journey. You love becoming more of the person God created you to be, so that you "may be mature and complete, not lacking anything" (James 1:4). *And,* even liking a new you will feel awkward and unfamiliar for a while!

> Bestow on them a crown of beauty
> instead of ashes,
> the oil of joy
> instead of mourning,
> and a garment of praise
> instead of a spirit of despair. (Isa. 61:3)

▶ Turn to the Gentle Assignments section on page 179 for further reflection.

160

12

Trauma and Transformation

From struggle comes strength. When we are broken, we are not less than or diminished. We have taken a different form . . . the beauty, grandeur and strength come when we put our lives back together and reveal our new selves to the world.

Richard Tedeschi and Bret Moore

REMEMBER BOTH/AND THEOLOGY? I have been italicizing *and* throughout this book to emphasize how different it is to think this way. Black-and-white thinking—either/or theology—promotes only one truth at a time. For instance, here is what you could say if you were traumatized by life and looked at only the painful part: "It was horrible. It was hard. I did not see anything valuable in this experience. I would not want anyone to have to go through this."

Or you focus only on the positive change you experienced from going through something difficult: "I have grown so much from this trauma. I would never have known how strong I was if I had not gone through this trial. It changed the person I am."

The complete truth, though, is that *both* of those thoughts are true. "I have been through something traumatic. It was painful. I was hurting. It was hard to see the value in that experience at first. *And* I became a different person, having lived through it. I changed. Good came . . . eventually." This is both/and theology. This is both/and thinking. You do not need to negate one thought to make another true. They both can be true at the same time.

Let's conclude with another both/and truth: trauma *and* transformation can coexist. These life experiences that create so much pain and loss can cause tremendous confusion, uncertainty, hopelessness, and despair. *And*, with enough support, you can grow individually, relationally, and spiritually through them. Trauma does not need to lead to tragedy. Trauma can be transformational. Clinical research has validated this, and ongoing research of traumatic life experiences, including loss of loved ones, serious illness, incest, war, natural disasters, and accidents, shows that growth occurs following these trials.[1] My research has also validated this for women who have been relationally betrayed, as did my personal journey through betrayal trauma.

The truth about trauma and transformation can be found in God's both/and theology. We read it over and over in the Bible. Let's look once more at what James tells us:

> Consider it pure joy . . . whenever you face trials of many kinds, because you know that the testing of your faith develops perseverance. Let perseverance finish its work so that you may be mature and complete, not lacking anything. (James 1:2–4)

God is much less interested in right circumstances than he is in right responses. He wants to refine and transform our character, not necessarily change the circumstances of our lives. We do not always know the depth of our character until we respond to pressure or pain. God knows that we can all look extremely kind and loving when things are going well. As Rick Warren said in *The Purpose*

Driven Life, "We learn things about God in suffering that we can't learn any other way."[2] I would add that we also learn things about ourselves in suffering that we can't learn any other way.

We do not, by nature, consider suffering a privilege. We do not enjoy pain. *And* maybe we can use it to build our character, change our priorities, grow our patience and dependence on God, allow others to serve us as we serve them, and find something to be thankful for in all situations—eventually. Out of suffering there is gain. It is the paradox of adversity: the struggle initiates growth.

I think about all the natural tendencies we human beings have in comparison to the supernatural characteristics God wants to develop in us. When we look for purpose in our pain, we have the opportunity to mature through building these qualities of character.

Natural	Supernatural
Desiring to be strong in everything.	Accepting weakness as a strength.
Speeding up life.	Slowing life down and growing patience.
Being independent and self-sufficient.	Depending on God.
Making people "pay" and getting revenge.	Forgiving others' trespasses.
Trying harder and harder.	Surrendering to God.
Avoiding pain.	Embracing pain: *What can I learn?*
Getting angry with hardship.	Being thankful for what you learn from trials.
Identifying success as growing assets.	Identifying success as giving assets away.
Doing anything to get ahead.	Taking the high road, doing what is right.
Feeling guilty.	Living in forgiveness.
Hiding bad behavior and mistakes.	Confessing and owning failure and sin.
Being silent about difficult emotions.	Being authentic.
Loving only what is lovable.	Loving others unconditionally.
Hating mistakes and bad decisions.	Creating humbleness and having empathy for others.
Living with anxiety and fear.	Living with peace and calm.

That is a long list of character traits to develop, and there are more. Would you be more inclined to accept trials in your life if you knew they could lead to your sanctification? What a privilege to know you can be on an important journey of growing these supernatural qualities. Miranda said to me one day in counseling, "God did not give me my story to put in my pocket!" She has used her story to grow and grow and grow, and to serve others today who have similar stories.

Elizabeth Kübler-Ross was a well-known researcher and writer about death and grieving. She saw many people in adversity and crisis. She articulately describes beautiful people in these words:

> The most beautiful people we have known are those who have known defeat, known suffering, known struggle, known loss, and have found their way out of the depths. These people have an appreciation, a sensitivity, and an understanding of life that fills them with compassion, gentleness, and a deep, loving concern. Beautiful people do not just happen.[3]

I am only eighteen months from the death of my beloved husband, my soul mate and ministry partner for nearly fifty years. People ask me regularly how I am doing. I always give a both/and response. "Deep down inside me, it is well with my soul, *and* I still feel great sorrow and loneliness at times." That feels authentic to say. It is all right to feel all those things. My heart feels congruent. It allows me to open myself to what is next and take lessons of change and loss with me. I am learning new skills and seeing my character traits refined. I feel God smiling and know he knows my pain too. I also know that while on this earth, there will be even more hard experiences.

Each time I face something difficult, I feel more equipped and more certain of these truths:

God is with me and for me.
God will not waste my pain.

Surrendering *my* understanding and *my* timing is hard.
God has a plan to prosper me . . . eventually.
Trauma *and* transformation coexist.

Blessed is the one who perseveres under trial because, having stood the test, that person will receive the crown of life that the Lord has promised to those who love him. (James 1:12)

Acknowledgments

I first want to thank my gracious editor, Vicki Crumpton, for extending my original deadline for writing this book. I signed the contract before my husband passed away, and I had no idea how difficult it would be to write while grieving that tremendous loss. Vicki evidently did, and from the very start she gave me the space to write when it felt right. And eventually it did.

I also want to thank the amazing team I work with at Faithful & True, my counseling center. With their expertise and confidence in providing the workshops, groups, and counseling we have offered for many years, they have carried on while I took time away to rest and write. I have never doubted that all would be well in our season of loss of Mark and his leadership, followed by the challenges of COVID-19.

My children, Sarah, Jon, and Ben, have been a source of great joy and strength. They continue to support my talents to teach, counsel, and write. While their dad was outstanding in all these ways, I have so appreciated their belief that I can carry on that legacy with my gifts. They have been my constant encouragers.

My brother Dan Wolter, my niece Lindsay Martin, and my dear friend Mary Munger gave me the precious gift of their time to read through my manuscript and offer opinions. While they have not had the same trials as I have, they said they learned ways to grow from anything difficult. That was music to my ears! They confirmed my hope for this book.

I want to thank Dee Vodicka for the eight years of her time she gave to cofacilitate a women's group with me. She took notes of my teaching throughout those years, and we were discussing writing this book together. When she and her husband moved back to their home in Atlanta and Mark's cancer was diagnosed, our joint effort never happened. Her ongoing belief in my work, however, gave me confidence on those days when I questioned the worth of another book about pain. You will never know how valuable your encouragement has been, Dee.

At the anniversary of Mark's passing, a colleague and friend of Mark's and mine, John Thomas, offered to help with anything I needed. The Spirit immediately urged me to ask if he would critique my manuscript. John is a professor of psychology and an author himself, and I knew this was a big ask. I still get teary-eyed when I think of this story today, for he immediately said he would be honored to. What a gift that has been.

Elizabeth Griffin and David Delmonico are colleagues and friends who spearheaded my research project on posttraumatic growth. They contributed endless hours to me and this important work. And even more than their expertise in addiction and psychology, I appreciate their friendship that has surrounded me in my current season of being a widow.

I've had the privilege to counsel and lead groups for hundreds of women. I witnessed many of them move from the heartbreaking devastation of relationship betrayal to thriving. It was hard work for them, and it took time. Their stories of transformation go with me in all my counseling and writing. They provide the ongoing evidence of hope in all our trials. They are the reason I continue to do what I do. I love seeing changed lives. Thank you, dear women.

My mom is 101 years old now, and she encourages and affirms all of my endeavors with such sweetness, including this new book.

She asked me every time we talked how my writing was going and if it was finished yet! She is a willing participant when I practice my "tools" with her. She reminds me that it is never too late to change how we live so that we have more peace in our days.

I thank my late husband, Mark, who by his own example of being authentic about his story of addiction opened the path for me to share my story more readily. I know my sharing did not depend upon that, and yet it made it so much easier. His writing, teaching, and counseling all started with his story of brokenness. His life was a portrait of how he transformed that pain to be the person God created him to be and to use his story to help others. I dearly miss your input and your encouragement of this book, Mark. I am quite sure you are smiling down from heaven on a project you so believed in.

I am most thankful for God and all he is teaching me through adversity. He shows up in extraordinary ways to remind me of his presence. He moves me to my passion and purpose in times of joy, and he moves me to learning and change in times of hardship. I am learning to trust his timing and trust him with all the desires of my heart—even more so today.

Gentle Assignments

A few gentle assignments are listed here for you to start healing and growing from a trial or trauma in your life.

Additional questions for your reflection or group study are available at www.faithfulandtrue.com/resources/gentleassignments.

Chapters 1 & 2: The Pain of Being in Pain

1. Start with the Basics

Choose one of these physical components to focus on this week: sleep, food, exercise, or money. Which one disturbs your peace the most? Then make a small next right step. For instance, if you are not sleeping well, what can you do to improve your sleep, or who might you see for help?

2. Slow Down

What is something you could eliminate or simplify in your life right now so that you could accept a slower pace for a while?

3. Find Companionship

Will you think about one or two safe people with whom you can share your whole story? One of those might be a counselor. What makes a woman safe for you? Eventually, you may grow this list to a few more safe women. How will you find more safe women for your list?

4. Invest in Yourself

If you pay attention to when you are irritable, exhausted, or resentful, I think you will find a slice of self-care that is calling to you! Ask it what it needs. Maybe you need time alone. Maybe you want to get away and read. Maybe you need some women who understand your journey. Maybe you need a break from parenting. Maybe you need a warm bath and a nap. Explore your core beliefs about self-care, or taking care of yourself.

5. Create a POYO

Walk around your entire house—peeking into closets, storage areas, the basement, nooks under staircases, any unused rooms or spaces—and consider where you might find a Place of Your Own. You will know it is right because you'll have this burst of energy or passion that emerges. *Aha! I think this will do.* Where will your POYO be located?

6. Explore the Concept of Both/And

As you listen to yourself or someone else talk, take a sentence that included *but* and make it into a both/and statement by using the word *and* instead.

7. Remember the Slinky and the Roller Coaster

Think about what your emotions or feelings have been like since you experienced a traumatic betrayal or life experience. Name the feelings that come and go when you are going through this trauma.

8. Learn to Grieve Well

Make a list of some of the losses you have experienced in your life. Some may have been intentional (a family move, a change in jobs, a friend moving away), and some may have been a surprise (the discovery of infidelity, a pandemic, a frightening diagnosis, the death of a loved one).

Chapters 3 & 4: Surviving or Thriving

1. Take Responsibility for Yourself

What modeling have you had in your family of origin about taking responsibility for your well-being?

2. Live Authentically

Do you like being around people who are authentic? Why? Will you start by watching yourself and noticing when you do not believe your words or actions match the "real you"? Just make note of it in your journal. It is something you can slowly work on!

3. See Your Feelings As Messengers

In a journal or notebook, jot down what you are feeling four times a day—at breakfast, lunch, dinner, and bedtime. Use feeling words other than *good* or *fine* or *tired*. This can be hard, because these words are used by so many people. This first step is just getting used to noticing and naming your feelings, expanding your emotional vocabulary as you do so.

4. Ask Yourself: How Do I Cope?

Name some of the behaviors or substances you use to exit or minimize feelings you do not want to feel (coping). They may be on the list in chapter 4, or you may list other things that fit you. The possibilities are endless.

5. Identify and Communicate Your Needs

Are you good at asking for what you need? If so, how were you encouraged to do that? If not, what prevented you from asking?

6. Explore Your Motivation

Write down several examples of making decisions based on your motivation to take care of yourself.

7. Live Intentionally

Do you describe yourself as a reactive person or a proactive one? What are some examples?

8. Ask Yourself: What Disturbs My Peace?

Think about a situation when you were not able to change something, then try using the Serenity Prayer. Name what you *cannot* change. Name what you *can* change. What, if anything, will you need to surrender to God?

9. Take the Next Right Step

What Scriptures can you find to encourage you to stay present to your worries or concerns today?

10. Make Choices

What can you do if you struggle to know what your choices are in a given situation?

Chapters 5 & 6: Exploring You— The Person You Take Everywhere

1. Be a Gentle Observer

Can you take your gentle observer with you when you notice others or yourself and just watch and not judge? List a few times you have noticed without judging. How did that feel?

2. Consider Your Worth

Find a picture of yourself when you were four or five years old and put it in a beautiful frame. Put it where you will see that little girl several times a day. Notice what you are feeling and thinking when you see her. Start by telling her what you like about her as you pass by.

3. Have the Courage to Be Imperfect

Do you struggle with perfectionism? In what areas of your life does it show up? What do you think you sacrifice in taking time to do things perfectly?

4. Examine Your Cabinet of Core Beliefs

Make a list of your beliefs when you were young using these categories: money, the value of men, the value of women, success, religion and spirituality, trusting men, trusting women, having needs, men who are unfaithful in marriage, accepting help, providing help, privacy, anger, lying, having fun, and showing emotions.

5. Find Yourself

Do you have trouble knowing who you are—what you feel or need or like? If so, where might you begin to practice talking about your feelings, your needs, and your likes?

6. Consider Your Brain Health

Do you struggle with anxiety, depression, obsessive-compulsive disorder (OCD), attention deficit disorder (ADD or ADHD), sleep disorders, or posttraumatic stress disorder (PTSD)? If so, which ones? What help have you had to improve your brain health?

7. Where Do You Rev?

When you think back to your earlier life experiences, what events, people, or circumstances created a lack of safety for you?

8. How Do You Respond When You Are Angry?

Think about a few situations this last week that made you angry. Write them down in your journal. Then think about what you needed in each situation and write that down next to the situation. How can you get some of those needs met?

Chapters 7 & 8: What Is It Like to Be in Relationship with You?

1. Ask Yourself: How Safe Am I?

People you are around may be doing or saying something that creates unsafety. Do you recognize how you might not be safe? List examples in these categories:

Verbally
Physically
Sexually
Spiritually
Financially

Decide what one next right step you might take to create safety for yourself.

2. Practice Do-Overs

Name a situation with another person that did not go well. Practice writing out what you would say or do if you could have a "do-over."

3. Check Out Your Perceptions

The next time you get annoyed by or are resentful about something, notice what your perception is. What are you thinking? What is "the story in your head"? (For example, when a car sped past me, weaving in and out of traffic and ending up two cars ahead of me at the light, the story in my head was, *Everyone is in such a hurry these days!*)

4. Ask Yourself: How Do I Handle Conflict?

What did you learn in your early home life about managing conflict (or managing differences)?

176

5. Consider the Turtle and the Hammer

Do you recognize you can be a Turtle or a Hammer in your marriage? Which one? Name a situation where your Turtle or Hammer shows up.

6. Ask Yourself: Am I a Partner or a Parent?

What does it mean to you to be a partner in your relationship rather than a parent?

7. Become a Stand-Alone Person

How would you describe the difference between *wanting* to be in relationship rather than *needing* to be in relationship? Which is emotionally healthier?

8. Embrace Authentic Emotional Intimacy

Do you want to be emotionally intimate—capable of sharing what you are feeling, thinking, and needing or desiring? Why is that important?

9. Accept Handicaps

Are you able to accept your physical and emotional limitations? Your spouse's? Why or why not?

10. Work toward Unconditional Love

What can you do when you don't receive unconditional love from your spouse?

Chapter 9: A New Trust

1. Trusting Others

In thinking as far back as you can, who has broken your trust? List the situation, your age, and how your trust was broken.

2. Trusting Yourself

Do you trust yourself to make decisions? Why or why not?

How have you experienced the Spirit within helping you with direction and decisions?

3. Trusting God

What experiences have you had that grew your trust in God? What has broken your trust with God?

Chapter 10: Everything Cries Holy—Letting Life Teach You

1. Everything Cries Holy

When has God seemed to want to work on changing something in you (e.g., being impatient, being controlling, feeling inadequate, being judgmental, feeling unloved), and he delivered several opportunities to do so?

2. Loneliness versus Solitude

How would you explain the difference between loneliness and solitude?

3. Ahas Are Personal

Do you remember having an aha lately? When did it happen, and what was the aha?

4. Stadium Seating

When you are going through something traumatic or difficult, I would say you have a front-row seat—or you are in the game. Do you try to make big decisions when you are in that place? If so, why?

5. God Won't Waste Your Pain

List any experiences when you endured a failure of some kind, or a hardship, and it eventually led to something good.

6. Surrender, Surrender, Surrender!

Describe a situation when you did all that you knew you could do and then surrendered it to God. What happened when you did that?

Chapter 11: Liking the New You—Transforming

1. The Posttraumatic Growth Inventory

Take the Posttraumatic Growth Inventory (appendix D). List the date and your total score. Save your results and take it again after you have been working on the practical steps to your well-being—maybe in six months.

Did you see changes in the results? In what areas are you growing/changing the most?

2. The Intimacy Skills Inventory

Take the Intimacy Skills Inventory (appendix E). List the date and your total score. Save your results and take it again after you have been working on the practical steps to your well-being—maybe in six months.

Did you see changes in the results? In what areas are you growing/changing the most?

3. The Fruit of the Spirit (Gal. 5:22–23)

Write a sentence or two about each Fruit and how you assess your ability to live with that Fruit. Is it regularly part of your life? Sometimes? Rarely? Would you like to work on growing in the character of that Fruit?

Love	Patience	Faithfulness
Joy	Kindness	Gentleness
Peace	Goodness	Self-control

Chapter 12: Trauma and Transformation

Your Last Gentle Assignment

Looking at the table comparing natural and supernatural characerics (page 163), which supernatural characteristics do you claim or are working on claiming?

Are you willing to get more professional help if despair has continued after a traumatic experience? Where or with whom might you get help?

Do you like using *and* to describe embracing the despair and growth that are experienced in adversity? Why or why not? Practice creating several both/and sentences from difficult experiences in your life.

List character traits or parts of yourself that contribute to the beautiful person you are. If you are having difficulty, ask a trusted friend to help you.

Feelings

Get to Know Who You Are on the Inside

*Notice that *good* and *fine* are not on the list.

Mad	Sad	Bad	Glad	Afraid
Annoyed	Hurt	Guilty	Content	Fearful
Angry	Vulnerable	Ashamed	Satisfied	Scared
Irritated	Blue	Defective	Happy	Nervous
Aggravated	Unhappy	Less than	Tender	Frightened
Frustrated	Depressed	Rejected	Excited	Apprehensive
Agitated	Sorrowful	Unworthy	Optimistic	Worried
Furious	Discouraged	Unlovable	Grateful	Terrified
Disgusted	Disheartened	Unacceptable	Loving	Unsafe
Outraged	Lonely	Betrayed	Fulfilled	Insecure
Enraged	Disappointed	Helpless	Peaceful	Anxious
Fed up	Hopeless	Inadequate	Hopeful	Confused

Erik Erikson's Stages of Development

If one or more of these stages was not healthily developed as a young person, you may notice that you have struggles with those tasks as an older adult.[1]

1. **Trust vs. Mistrust** (infancy, birth–18 months)
   When successful, infants receive constant and reliable care that develops a sense of trust. This trust will go with them into other relationships to produce a sense of security. When trust is not met consistently, suspicion and anxiety may develop.

2. **Autonomy vs. Shame** (toddlerhood, 18 months–3 years)
   When successful, children develop a sense of personal control over physical skills and a sense of independence. It leads to confidence in their ability to survive in the world. When children are criticized or overly controlled, they begin to feel inadequate, can become dependent upon others, lack self-esteem, and feel a sense of shame or doubt about their abilities.

3. **Initiative vs. Guilt** (young childhood, 3–5 years)
When successful, children practice initiating, creating, and asking questions through their play with others. With support, this opportunity develops initiative and creates security in leading others and making decisions. If there is too much criticism or control, children's initiative can be squelched, which can lead to guilt.
Some balance between initiative and guilt is healthy.

4. **Industry (Competence) vs. Inferiority** (middle childhood, 5–12 years)
At this stage, children are learning specific skills in school. Approval of peers becomes more important. Affirmation from parents and significant adults contributes to children feeling competent and proud of abilities. Not gaining specific skills deemed successful by society or parents (e.g., being athletic) may develop a sense of inferiority. Some failure builds modesty and is helpful to growth.

5. **Identity vs. Role Confusion** (adolescence, 12–18 years)
This stage allows adolescents to search for their sense of self and personal identity through exploration of values, beliefs, and goals. There is a great need to belong in society. Exploration of both sexual and occupational identities is involved.

6. **Intimacy vs. Isolation** (young adulthood, 18–40 years)
The major challenge of this stage is building loving, close relationships. There is more sharing and vulnerability of oneself. Avoiding intimacy and fearing commitment can lead to isolation, loneliness, and possibly depression.

7. **Generativity vs. Stagnation** (middle adulthood, 40–65 years)
Individuals experience a need to create or nurture things that will outlast them. Feeling productive through raising a family, contributing to society, engaging in community

activities, working—all are part of the bigger picture. Success leads to feelings of usefulness and meaning, while failure results in shallow involvement in life.

8. **Ego Integrity vs. Despair** (late adulthood, 65+ years) This stage is a time to contemplate one's life and accomplishments. Success will lead to feeling one has a life of integrity, while failure will lead to regret, despair, and bitterness.

APPENDIX C

FANOS Check-In

FANOS is a daily five-minute check-in with your spouse to practice emotional intimacy . . . from the Greek word that means "to shine" or "to reveal."[1] Take turns as each spouse checks in with the other about these things.

After the first spouse is finished, the second spouse may check in. Do not interrupt, correct, or ask questions until you are both finished. If you have time and want to talk further, you can do so after you have both shared your FANOS and agree to take more time for a longer conversation.

Feelings—state your feelings (not your thoughts!).

Affirmation—give your spouse an affirmation or say "thank you" for something your spouse did.

Needs—ask for something you need, not necessarily from your spouse. (Remember that sometimes your need will not be met.)

Own something—say you are sorry or apologize for something you said or did that was hurtful to your spouse.

Sobriety—the addict will check in with his/her spouse about his/her sobriety. If sobriety is no longer an issue, you may each choose something you want to change (such as habitual TV watching, rage, withdrawal, sarcasm, unhealthy eating) for your spiritual growth or self-care, and check in about how your progress is going with that issue.

For example,

F: I am feeling nervous today about a big meeting I need to attend.

A: Thank you for being so patient with me while I have been preparing for this.

N: I would love to just unwind tonight by going out to dinner—would you be willing to get a sitter so we can go out alone?

O: I really snapped at you when you were trying to tell me something, and I apologize for that.

S: (For the addict) I want you to know that I am sober today. (For the spouse) I am working on being safer with my anger. I am still yelling at you and the kids sometimes, and I want to stop that behavior.

The Posttraumatic Growth Inventory

What Growth Do You See in Your Journey?

By Richard G. Tedeschi and Lawrence G. Calhoun[1]

I recommend taking this inventory before you begin working through your adversity or traumatic life event. After you have been working on some of the practical ideas in this book for six months, take it again to see how you are growing.

For each item, give yourself a score from 1–5.
(5 = "I experience this to a very great degree."
and 1 = "I did not experience this at all.")

I know better that I can handle difficulties.	
I have more compassion for others.	

I have a stronger religious faith.	
I discovered I am stronger than I thought I was.	
I am more likely to change things that need changing.	
I have a better understanding of spiritual matters.	
I am more willing to express my emotions.	
I have a greater appreciation for the value of my life.	
I put more efforts into my relationships.	
I have a greater feeling of self-reliance.	
I changed my priorities about what is important in life.	
I established a new path for my life.	
I more clearly see that I can count on people in times of trouble.	
I am better able to accept the ways things work out.	
I have greater emotional intimacy with my spouse/partner.	
I can better appreciate each day.	
I am better able to do things with my life.	
New opportunities are available that would not have been otherwise.	
I better accept needing others.	
I learned a great deal about how wonderful people are.	
I have a greater sense of closeness with others.	
I developed new interests.	

DATE: _____ TOTAL SCORE: _____

APPENDIX E

The Intimacy Skills Inventory

What Growth Do You See in Your Journey?

By Debbie Laaser, MA, LMFT[1]

I recommend taking this inventory before you begin working through your adversity or traumatic life event. After you have been working on some of the practical ideas in this book for six months, take it again to see how you are growing.

For each question, give yourself a score from 1–5.
(5 = "I experience this to a very great degree."
and 1 = "I do not experience this at all.")

I know I always have choices.	
I more easily identify behaviors I need or want to change.	
I take responsibility for my own feelings, thoughts, behaviors, and happiness.	
I create safety for myself.	
I have safe people in my life.	

When I make mistakes, I readily own what I did wrong.	
My life has significance.	
I can see different perspectives—I'm not black-and-white about things.	
I take care of my emotional, physical, and spiritual needs.	
I can allow others to be different than I am.	
I know what I feel and can articulate my feelings to others.	
I have courage to be imperfect.	
I like who I am and consider myself worthy.	
I am resourceful.	
I trust myself.	
I state my needs and desires clearly.	
I can accept the limitations of others.	
I am proactive rather than reactive.	
I can enjoy the moment without getting overly focused on the past or the future.	
I trust others.	
I do not personalize others' behaviors and words.	
I can wait for resolution of issues.	

DATE: _____ TOTAL SCORE: _____

Introduction

1. Richard G. Tedeschi and Lawrence G. Calhoun, "Posttraumatic Growth: Conceptual Foundations and Empirical Evidence," *Psychological Inquiry* 15, no. 1 (2004): 1.

Chapter 1 The Pain of Being in Pain

1. Steven Joseph, *What Doesn't Kill Us: The New Psychology of Posttraumatic Growth* (New York: Basic Books, 2011), 10–15.

2. Joseph, *What Doesn't Kill Us*, 11.

3. Joseph, *What Doesn't Kill Us*, 12.

4. Joseph, *What Doesn't Kill Us*, 37.

5. Joseph, *What Doesn't Kill Us*, 14.

6. Richard G. Tedeschi and Lawrence G. Calhoun, "The Posttraumatic Growth Inventory: Measuring the Positive Legacy of Trauma," *Journal of Traumatic Stress* 9, no. 3 (1996): 455–71.

7. Debra Laaser et al., "Posttraumatic Growth in Relationally Betrayed Women," *Journal of Marital and Family Therapy* 43 (2017): 435–47.

8. Joseph, *What Doesn't Kill Us*, xvi–xvii.

9. Politico Staff, "Getting There: Maya Angelou," *Politico*, May 29, 2014, https://www.politico.com/story/2014/05/getting-there-maya-angelou-107195.

10. Ronnie Janoff-Bulman, *Shattered Assumptions: Towards a New Psychology of Trauma* (New York: Free Press, 1992), 51.

11. Janoff-Bulman, *Shattered Assumptions*, 52.

12. Laaser et al., "Posttraumatic Growth in Relationally Betrayed Women," 436.

13. Larry Crabb, *Shattered Dreams: God's Unexpected Pathway to Joy* (Colorado Springs: Waterbrook Press, 2001), 4.

Chapter 2 Getting Practical When You Are in Pain

1. Sarah Young, *Jesus Calling* (Nashville: Thomas Nelson, 2004), 75.

2. Sarah Susanka, *The Not So Big House: A Blueprint for the Way We Really Live* (Newtown, CT: Taunton Press, 1998), 59.

3. Jim Collins, *Built to Last: Successful Habits of Visionary Companies* (New York: HarperCollins, 1994), 43–44.

4. Sue Monk Kidd, *The Secret Life of Bees* (New York: Penguin, 2002), 97–98.

Chapter 3 Surviving or Thriving

1. Rick Warren, *The Purpose Driven Life: What on Earth Am I Here For?* (Grand Rapids: Zondervan, 2002), 194.

Chapter 4 Practical Steps to Move from Surviving to Thriving

1. Young, *Jesus Calling*, 113.

2. Reinhold Niebuhr, from a sermon at Heath Evangelical Union Church in Heath, Massachusetts, 1943.

3. Viktor E. Frankl, *Man's Search for Meaning* (Boston: Beacon Press, 1946), 66.

Chapter 5 Exploring You—The Person You Take Everywhere

1. Tim Clinton and Gary Sibcy, *Attachments: Why You Love, Feel and Act the Way You Do* (Nashville: Thomas Nelson, 2002), 23.

Chapter 6 Practical Steps to Exploring You

1. Henri J. M. Nouwen, *Life of the Beloved: Spiritual Living in a Secular World* (New York: Crossroad, 1992), 31.

2. Nouwen, *Life of the Beloved*, 31.

3. Alfred Adler, *The Lexicon of Adlerian Psychology: 106 Terms Associated with the Individual Psychology of Alfred Adler*, 2nd ed. (Port Townsend, WA: Adlerian Psychology Associates, 2007), 19.

4. G. K. Chesterton, *Orthodoxy* (repr. San Francisco: Ignatius, 1995), 127.

5. Daniel G. Amen, *Change Your Brain, Change Your Life: The Breakthrough Program for Conquering Anxiety, Depression, Obsessiveness, Anger, and Impulsiveness* (New York: Three Rivers Press, 1998), 7.

6. Daniel G. Amen, *The End of Mental Illness: How Neuroscience Is Transforming Psychiatry and Helping Prevent or Reverse Mood and Anxiety Disorders, ADHD, Addictions, PTSD, Psychosis Personality Disorders, and More* (Carol Stream, IL: Tyndale Momentum, 2020), 61.

Chapter 8 Practical Steps to Examine Your Relationship

1. Mark Laaser and Debbie Laaser, *Seven Desires: Looking Past What Separates Us to Learn What Connects Us* (Grand Rapids: Zondervan, 2008), 17–41.

2. Erik H. Erikson, *Childhood and Society* (London: Vintage, 1995), 221–47.

Chapter 9 A New Trust

1. Mark Laaser and Debbie Laaser, *A Toolkit for Growth: Practical Recovery Tools for Individuals & Couples* (Minneapolis: Hillcrest Media Group, 2017), 16–24.

2. Debra Laaser, *Shattered Vows: Hope and Healing for Women Who Have Been Sexually Betrayed* (Grand Rapids: Zondervan, 2008), 184–85.

3. Laaser and Laaser, *Toolkit for Growth*, 57.

Chapter 10 Everything Cries Holy—Letting Life Teach You

1. Henri J. M. Nouwen, *Reaching Out: The Three Movements of the Spiritual Life* (New York: Doubleday, 1975), 25–30.

2. Rainer Maria Rilke, as quoted in Martha W. Hickman, *Healing After Loss: Daily Meditations for Working Through Grief* (New York: HarperCollins, 1994), entry for May 9.

3. *NIV Life Application Study Bible* (Grand Rapids: Zondervan, 1991), 942.

4. See Debra Laaser, *Threads of Curiosity* (blog), https://faithfulandtrue.com/blog/debbies-blog.

5. George MacDonald, as quoted in Hickman, *Healing After Loss*, entry for October 13.

Chapter 11 Liking the New You—Transforming

1. Tedeschi and Calhoun, "The Posttraumatic Growth Inventory," 455–71.

Chapter 12 Trauma and Transformation

1. Tedeschi and Calhoun, "The Posttraumatic Growth Inventory," 455–56.

2. Warren, *The Purpose Driven Life*, 194.

3. Elisabeth Kübler-Ross, *Death: The Final Stage of Growth* (New York: Touchstone, 1975), 96.

Appendix B Erik Erikson's Stages of Development

1. Adapted from Erik Erikson, *Childhood and Society* (New York: Norton, 1950).

Appendix C FANOS Check-In

1. Originally published in Debra Laaser, *Shattered Vows: Hope and Healing for Women Who Have Been Sexually Betrayed* (Grand Rapids: Zondervan, 2008). Used by permission.

Appendix D The Posttraumatic Growth Inventory

1. Adapted from Richard G. Tedeschi and Lawrence G. Calhoun, "The Posttraumatic Growth Inventory: Measuring the Positive Legacy of Trauma," *Journal of Traumatic Stress* 9, no. 3 (1996): 455–71. Used by permission.

Appendix E The Intimacy Skills Inventory

1. Originally published in Debra Laaser et al., "Posttraumatic Growth in Relationally Betrayed Women," *Journal of Marital and Family Therapy* 43 (2007), https://faithfulandtrue.com/wp-content/uploads/2020/01/POSTTRAUMATIC-GROWTH-IN-RELATIONALLY-BETRAYED-WOMEN-by-Debbie-L.pdf. Used by permission.

Debra Laaser, MA, is a Licensed Marriage and Family Therapist and was involved in recovery with her husband, Mark, for over thirty years. After Mark's passing in 2019, she became the director of their counseling center, Faithful & True, treating men struggling with sexual addiction and their spouses. Debbie has facilitated therapy groups, individual counseling, and intensives for betrayed wives for over twenty years. She authored *Shattered Vows*, co-authored with Mark *Seven Desires* and *A Toolkit for Growth*, and published research, "Posttraumatic Growth in Relationally Betrayed Women." She lives in Minneapolis and enjoys life with her three adult children, their respective spouses and spouse-to-be, and her four grandchildren.

ARE YOU STRUGGLING WITH THE
Trauma of Relational Betrayal?

Faithful & True is a Christian counseling center cofounded by Dr. Mark and Debbie Laaser. It is located in Eden Prairie, Minnesota, and specializes in the treatment of sexual addiction for men, support for their spouses, and guidance for couples who have experienced relational betrayal.

Find Sexual Integrity in a Fallen World

The Faithful & True Podcast brings practical discussions to men struggling with sexual addiction and their partners. A vast offering of topics contributes to listeners' well-being and growth to become the people God calls them to be. You can find *The Faithful & True Podcast* wherever you listen to podcasts, or you can watch the podcasts on YouTube by searching for *The Faithful & True Podcast*.

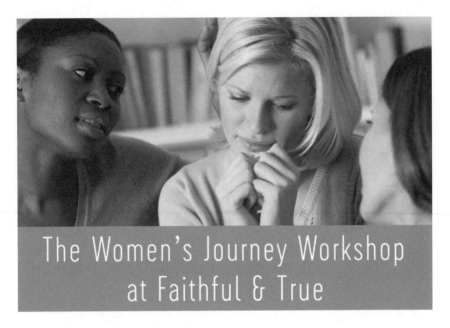

The Women's Journey Workshop
at Faithful & True

Join us for a three-day event where women experiencing the trauma of relational betrayal join professional leaders with similar stories. Participants will learn about grieving, finding safe people, identifying coping, understanding the components of sexual addiction, and living in truth. They will also discuss their "story"—what shaped and formed them—as well as learn how couples develop over time, explore trust-building, and create a plan for moving forward. Knowing that trauma can be transformed to healing and growth leaves participants with the gift of hope.

Learn more at **faithfulandtrue.com/workshops**